THE POPULIST CHALLENGE

THE
JAMES SPRUNT STUDIES
IN HISTORY
AND POLITICAL SCIENCE

*Published under the Direction of the
Departments of History and Political Science of
The University of North Carolina at Chapel Hill*

VOLUME 58

THE POPULIST CHALLENGE

ARGENTINE ELECTORAL BEHAVIOR

IN THE POSTWAR ERA

Lars Schoultz

THE UNIVERSITY OF NORTH CAROLINA PRESS

CHAPEL HILL AND LONDON

© 1983 The University of North Carolina Press
All rights reserved
Manufactured in the United States of America

Library of Congress Cataloging in Publication Data

Schoultz, Lars.
The populist challenge.

(The James Sprunt studies in history and political
science ; v. 58)
Bibliography: p.
Includes index.
1. Populism—Argentina. 2. Social classes—Argentina.
3. Argentina—Politics and government—1943–1955.
4. Argentina—Politics and government—1955–
5. Voting—Argentina. 6. Peronism. I. Title.
II. Series.
JL2031.S36 1983   982'.06   82-24831
ISBN 0-8078-5059-4

To Nils, Karina, and Jane

CONTENTS

CHAPTER 1
Populism and Social Mobilization in Latin America
3

CHAPTER 2
Populist Challenge and Liberal Response
11

CHAPTER 3
Peronist Electoral Support: A Multivariate Analysis
43

CHAPTER 4
Peronist Electoral Change: An Index of Fluidity
67

Conclusion
85

Methodological Appendix
97

Notes
117

Bibliography
125

Index
139

TABLES AND FIGURES

TABLES

2.1   Argentina's Foreign-Born Population: Males
Twenty Years Old and Over   16

2.2   Urban-Rural Population Distributions, 1947   17

2.3   Correlations between Occupation and Party Vote,
Federal Capital, 1942   23

2.4   Correlations between Occupation and Party Vote,
Federal Capital, 1942   24

2.5   Argentine Election Results, 1946–1973   26

2.6   Social Class: Pearson Correlations between
Occupation and the Peronist Vote, Federal
Capital, 1946   29

2.7   Social Class: Pearson Correlations between
Occupation and the Peronist Vote, Federal
Capital, 1946–1973   30

2.8   Social Class: Pearson Correlations between
Occupation and the Peronist Vote, Greater
Buenos Aires, 1946–1973   31

2.9   Socioeconomic Characteristics and Orientations
toward Peronism, 1965   32

2.10   Argentine Social Class Structure by Economic
Sector, 1947   33

3.1   Pearson Correlations between Population
Growth and the Peronist Vote, Greater
Buenos Aires, 1946–1973   47

3.2   Pearson Correlations between the Level of
Industrialization and the Peronist Vote,
Greater Buenos Aires, 1946–1973   49

3.3   Pearson Correlations between the Level of
Industrialization and the Peronist Vote, All
Argentine Counties, 1946–1965   51

3.4   Pearson Correlations between Industrial Growth
and the Peronist Vote, Greater Buenos Aires,
1946–1973   52

3.5   Pearson Correlations between Economic
       Satisfaction and the Peronist Vote, Greater
       Buenos Aires, 1946–1973   55
3.6   Pearson Correlations between Industrial Wage
       Increases and the Peronist Vote, Greater
       Buenos Aires, 1946–1973   57
3.7   Uncontrolled Multiple Regression of PERON on
       the Composite Independent Variables, Greater
       Buenos Aires   59
3.8   Path Coefficients for Figure 3.1   61
3.9   Proportional Components of the Relationship
       between Industrial Growth and the Peronist
       Vote, Greater Buenos Aires   63
4.1   Index of Fluidity   70
4.2   Pearson Correlations between Indicators of
       Social Class and the Index of Fluidity   72
4.3   Pearson Correlations between Indicators of the
       Level of Industrialization and the Index of
       Fluidity   74
4.4   Pearson Correlations between Indicators of the
       Quality of Industrialization and the Index of
       Fluidity   76
4.5   Pearson Correlations between Indicators of
       Demographic Instability and the Index of
       Fluidity   77
4.6   Pearson Correlations between Indicators of
       Economic Satisfaction and the Index of Fluidity   78
4.7   Pearson Correlations between Indicators of
       Industrial Growth and the Index of Fluidity   79
4.8   Greater Buenos Aires: Pearson Correlations of
       Selected Socioeconomic-Demographic
       Indicators with Percent Perón, 1946–1965   80–81
4.9   All Argentine Counties: Pearson Correlations of
       Selected Socioeconomic-Demographic
       Indicators with Percent Perón, 1946–1965   82–83
A1   Factor Score Coefficients and Component
       Variables of PERON   102
A2   Pearson Correlations between PERON and Its
       Component Variables   103
A3   Orthogonally (Varimax) Rotated Factor Matrix for
       All Independent Variables   106–7

A4   Orthogonally (Varimax) Rotated Factor Matrix for
     Demographic Variables   108
A5   Oblique Primary Factors of Nine Socioeconomic
     Variables   109
A6   Factor Score Coefficients and Component
     Variables of WORKING CLASS   110
A7   Factor Score Coefficients and Component
     Variables of POPULATION GROWTH   110
A8   Factor Score Coefficients and Component
     Variables of SATISFACTION   111
A9   Factor Score Coefficients and Component
     Variables of INDUSTRIAL GROWTH   111
A10 Factor Score Coefficients and Component
     Variables of INDUSTRY   112
A11 Partial Correlations between PERON and the
     Composite Independent Variables   113–14
A12 Independent Composite Variable Product-
     Moment Correlation Matrix   115

FIGURES

3.1 Six-Variable Causal Model: Paths from Industrial
     Growth to the Peronist Vote   60
3.2 Six-Variable Causal Model: Selected Paths from
     Industrial Growth to the Peronist Vote   64

THE POPULIST CHALLENGE

CHAPTER 1

POPULISM AND SOCIAL MOBILIZATION

IN LATIN AMERICA

Forty years have passed since a provident, ambitious colonel blessed with an infectious smile, an extraordinary political intuition, and only the beginning of a middle-aged paunch first strode to the center of Argentina's political stage. Today, the personal drama of Argentine populism is complete. The climax—the almost magical golden days when *El líder* and his captivating wife could appear on a balcony of the Casa de Gobierno and be deafened by the roar of delight from half a million *descamisados* gathered below in the Plaza de Mayo—passed into history with the revolution of 1955 or, perhaps, with Evita's death three years earlier. But the final act hardly finished then, however, for until his death in 1974 Juan Domingo Perón remained the protagonist in the Argentine political drama.

A degenerate to his enemies and a saint to his friends, Perón represented truly impressive political forces—in 1973 these counted as much as 60 percent of the vote in a highly fragmented political culture where minority leadership is the rule rather than the exception. Even in exile, Perón obviously inspired fear in his adversaries, providing the large Argentine military establishment with its most common form of gainful employment, the anti-Peronist coup d'etat. In the generally heated ambience of Argentine politics, Perón's ability to arouse and sustain intense political emotion marked him as no ordinary *caudillo*, although, to be sure, he was a *caudillo* in every sense of the word. But his political movement endures as more, perhaps much more, than the legacy of the typical strong-willed demagogue. Juan Perón has been dead for a decade, but Peronism still vies with the military for domination of the Argentine political system.

POPULISM IN LATIN AMERICA

The use of a single word to describe a complex system of thought and behavior necessarily involves a certain measure of ambiguity;

yet the level of intellectual obscurity reached by the concept of populism is unusually high. Although the word *populism* is a common descriptive term in discussions of political movements, no one has yet been able to distinguish a populist ideology from other conventional systems of political thought. As Judith Shklar writes:

> Populism is a very slippery term. Does it refer to anything more specific than a confused mixture of hostile attitudes? Is it simply an imprecise way of referring to all those who are neither clearly "left" nor "right"? Does the word not just cover all those who have been neglected by a historiography that can allow no ideological possibilities other than conservative, liberal, and socialist, and which oscillates between the pillars of "right" and "left" as if these were laws of nature? Is populism anything but a rebellion that has no visa to the capitals of conventional thought?[1]

Several attempts have been made to provide an acceptable definition of populism. Peter Wiles would attach the populist label to "any creed or movement based on the following premise: virtue resides in the simple people, who are the overwhelming majority, and in their collective traditions." Edward Shils would include those movements that recognize the supremacy of the will of the people over every other standard and desire a direct relationship between the people and their leaders, unmediated by institutions.[2] To accept either of these definitions is to agree with Peter Worsley that "populism is better regarded as an emphasis, a dimension of political culture in general, not simply as a particular kind of overall ideological system or type of organization."[3]

Populism may be more useful as an analytic category when employed for groups of political systems with somewhat similar cultural, social, and historical structures. This may be particularly true of Latin America, where populism is widely used to describe a variety of political movements. Even in Latin America, however, fundamental disagreement exists over the nature of populism. To the revolution-oriented Dale Johnson, populism represents little more than the skillful demagoguery of bourgeois elites appealing to "certain non–property holding sectors of the middle class, workers, and the enfranchised sectors of the urban mass who are able to control labor and popular organizations," while to the more moderate Torcuato Di Tella, populism stands as "the only force on the side of reform in Latin America."[4] Other scholars bent upon attacking certain Hispanic cultural characteristics find populism an easy target for their disapproval, for it "does not challenge the *status quo*: work patterns are not disturbed; a literary and legally trained intelligentsia does not have to venture into new specialized fields; a premium is still put on the manipulation of words and people rather than things."[5]

Specific definitions of populism in Latin America are rare. Alistair Hennessy refers only to the ideological aspects of populism when he terms it "an organizational weapon to synchronize divergent group interests" which may be descriptive of "any movement not based on a specific social class."[6] He would admit to the populist circle of political movements most predominantly urban, mass-manipulative political organizations that develop in opposition to Latin America's traditional upper-class parties. Di Tella's more precise definition also emphasizes the influence of social-class composition: "a political movement which enjoys the support of the mass of the urban working class and/or peasantry but which does not result from the autonomous organizational power of either of these two sectors. It is also supported by non-working-class sectors upholding an anti-*status quo* ideology."[7]

As these definitions suggest, virtually all discussions of Latin American populism neglect ideology and concentrate instead upon the movements' social-class composition. According to many scholars, mass support comes from social strata mobilized by the revolution of rising expectations—large groups of individuals who find their aspirations frustrated by an inflexible social structure and a relatively stagnant economic system. At times comprising. "an expanding middle class, intellectuals, students, factions of the military, and classes in ascendance such as newer entrepreneurs, organized labor, and the urban underclass" but traditionally composed only of the urban working class with limited middle-class support, these strata become a single "disposable mass" whose latent political power is ignored by traditional political actors.[8]

Given this tendency to focus upon the composition of populist movements, alongside the shortage of reliable data on mass political behavior in Latin America, the principal focus of most studies of Latin American populism has fallen by default upon elite analysis. Johnson associates populist leadership with elements from the upper or upper-middle classes intent upon the manipulation of the lower strata for the purpose of maintaining or expanding their own power.[9]

Other analyses emphasize elite recruitment by concentrating upon conditions that tend to facilitate the development of iconoclastic leadership elements. Of special interest is E. E. Hagen's time-honored concept of status incongruence, modified and offered by Di Tella as a critical explanatory variable.[10] Status incongruence is the subjective perception of disparities in individual social status when appraised by various criteria. "Impoverished aristocrats, newly rich businessmen not yet accepted in high society, and ethnic minorities, they all add to the possibilities for creating this type of individual and group. When social rigidities make it difficult for them to regain a balanced status situation, the incongruents develop resentments, brooding over new ideas and ways of changing things."[11] The effect of status incongruence is to create insecure, hostile individuals of relatively high social status who are unwilling to support existing social and political structures.

According to Di Tella, the union of incongruent elites and disposable masses, a union made feasible by a common dislike for the status quo, produces populist political movements. Without this type of elite leadership, popular discontent "would produce movements similar to the English Chartist agitation, the French anarcho-sindicalist movement, or simply a wave of wildcat strikes or some other anomic expression" of profound discontent.[12] The incongruent elites seek power in order to break the rigidities of traditional societies. In any case, mass support will not be forthcoming should principal elites be unable to project the traditional *patrón* personality and nurture a sense of elite-mass kinship based upon common grievances.[13]

Once these preconditions have been met, asserts Di Tella, the nature of populism's subsequent development depends upon the extent of the elites' estrangement from the existing political system. Briefly stated, the movement's degree of commitment to radical change is a function of the sheer number and the class origin of populist elites. If relatively few in number within their own social class, "they find themselves in an insecure position and may well develop authoritarian and emotional attitudes." The larger the extent of acceptance of the ideas of populist elites, the more moderate will be their ideology. As to their class origin, lower-middle-class leadership tends to accentuate the radical nature of populist movements more than upper-middle-class elites, but never beyond the point predetermined by the extent of elite acceptance. A lower-middle-class elite, for example, would never be successful in radicalizing to the point of violence a populist movement in a society where there is broad intraclass acceptance of elite goals.[14]

The result of this analysis is the delineation of several Latin American "sub-populisms." *Upper-middle-class* elites whose ideas are broadly accepted within their class will form multiclass integrative populist parties, while these same elites when supporting generally unpopular ideas will produce militaristic reform parties that are less moderate and perhaps occasionally prone to advocate the use of violence but that nonetheless are unwilling to attack a traditional society's basic values. The first type of populism is exemplifed by the Mexican PRI, while Rojas Pinilla's Colombian dictatorship from 1953 to 1957 approximates the second. Populist movements led by *lower-middle-class* elites whose views are broadly accepted within that class will produce a type of populism that is mildly reformist and less violent than militaristic reform populism, while lower-middle-class leaders whose ideas are attractive to only a small part of their class will develop social revolutionary movements. Respective examples would be the moderate *aprista* parties and the radical *fidelismo* of contemporary Cuba.[15]

Di Tella also suggests that significant structural deterrents hamper the emergence of populist movements in Latin America's comparatively developed societies. There the lower classes have had more experience in the construction of autonomous political structures, and, perhaps more important, the mass public and many of the potential populist elites have been co-opted by the wealth of a more prosperous society and the potential for individual upward social mobility. Despite these deterrents, ten of Di Tella's twenty-two examples of Latin American populism are concentrated in the four comparatively developed nations of Argentina, Cuba, Chile, and Venezuela.

Notwithstanding Di Tella's attempt to clarify the nature of populism in Latin America, it is probable that populism has become a residual category, a convenient depository for many nontraditional political movements that defy placement on our discipline's conventional left-right continuum. Even when restricted to a regional application, in this case to Latin America, populism serves only as a descriptive term for the increasingly large number of political parties which have emerged in recent decades to challenge traditional actors and organizations—the type of party John Martz would label as "modern." Certainly Martz's nomenclature is more appropriate if, in practice, populism is to be used to distinguish the old from the new.[16]

The basic problem of studies of Latin American populism is the emphasis upon elite behavior and especially the attempt to explain

a macropolitical phenomenon (the development of populist movements) with micropolitical variables (elite personality characteristics). In particular, the concept of status incongruence is wholly
inadequate. As relationships among modern people become increasingly complex, the opportunity for individuals to develop
some type of status incongruence increases commensurately. Few
people can be free of the doubts capable of producing such subjective feelings. Even if incongruence is assumed to be relatively more
widespread in certain modernizing societies—a doubtful assumption at best—Di Tella's analysis fails to specify the reasons why
middle- and upper-class incongruents become populist leaders. Is
it not probable that upwardly mobile incongruents would become
wary of serious challenges to the status quo once they had attained
a relatively high position within the existing system? Furthermore,
there is no reason to assume that those individuals who profess
antitraditional attitudes as a result of real or imagined status incongruence would necessarily become populists. Several other
types of movements, including a decidedly antipopular elitist tech-
nocracy—the bureaucratic-authoritarian model—are plausible
alternatives to populism.

Nearly two decades after Di Tella first adapted Hagen's concept
to Latin American politics, no empirical investigation has corrobo-
rated the relationship he posited between feelings of inferiority
and hostility stemming from status incongruence and the development of any type of elite behavior. In fact, elite recruitment studies
have tended to downgrade the importance of personality variables.
Kenneth Prewitt argues convincingly that the idea "that a personality variable is responsible for pushing persons into political ca-
reers is a dubious proposition. Personality traits may influence
relative success in politics or affect the style of leadership once
office is won, but to distinguish political power aspirants from the
indifferents on such traits is not supported by any data currently
available."[17] As a means of explaining the process of populist elite
recruitment, status incongruence is supported neither by logical
argument nor by empirical evidence.

SOCIAL MOBILIZATION, STRUCTURAL CHANGE, AND THE DEVELOPMENT OF POPULISM

Instead of labeling as "populist" all nontraditional political movements in Latin America and concentrating upon their subclassifi-

cation through the use of quasi-psychological analyses that few people are qualified to evaluate, we may be able to learn more about populism by focusing attention upon alterations in patterns of social interaction which occur during the process of modernization. More specifically, this book examines the thesis that inadequate responses by archaic political systems to the strains of social mobilization encourage the development of innovative, "popular" political movements.

As formulated by Karl Deutsch, social mobilization is defined as "the process in which major clusters of old social, economic, and psychological commitments are eroded or broken and people become available for new patterns of socialization and behavior."[18] This is a complex procedure that affects every fiber in the fabric of traditional societies.

> Social mobilization is a name given to an overall process of change which happens to substantial parts of the population in countries which are moving from traditional to modern ways of life. It denotes a concept which brackets together a number of more specific processes of change, such as changes of residence, of occupation, of social setting, of face-to-face associations, of institutions, roles, and ways of acting, of experiences and expectations, and finally of personal memories, habits and needs, including the need for new patterns of group affiliation and new images of personal identity. Singly, and even more in their cumulative impact, these changes tend to influence and sometimes to transform political behavior.[19]

To measure the extent and rate of social mobilization, Deutsch employs a number of readily available indicators, including per capita gross national product, percent of the population urbanized, size of media audiences, and literacy levels. Since he assumes that the relative importance of all the indicators is equal, each subprocess possesses equal influence upon the rate of social mobilization.

Perhaps the most widely recognized analysis of the implications of social mobilization in Latin America is Gino Germani's study of Argentine society.[20] Following Deutsch, Germani defines social mobilization as the psychosocial process whereby passive, traditional, "submerged" groups acquire their own norms and aspirations distinct from those fixed by preexisting rules.[21] Concentrating upon the political concomitants of predominantly lower-class mobilization, Germani notes its direct relationship to increased mass political participation, which in turn forces profound transformations in elite recruitment and elite functions, alters traditional channels of political communication, and eventually creates an entirely new range of demands for government services that can only be met by a dramatic expansion and reorientation of traditional structures.

The response of traditional political actors to these new demands will likely prove inadequate. The political strains induced by social mobilization apparently are highest during the intermediate stages of political and economic development, after a threshold of significance has been reached in the mobilization process but before traditional structures have been modified. The expanding, mobilized groups whose demands for political recognition are left unattended by an inflexible political structure form the bases of populist political movements. In the initial stages of social mobilization, these demands undoubtedly remain latent; migrants to urban centers, first-generation literates, and recent purchasers of transistor radios need time to adjust to their new environments.

Eventually, however, perhaps after one or more generations, this passive stage ends and newly mobilized groups begin to demand schools, employment, housing, and a host of other necessities. At the same time, though, the marginal status of the newly mobilized sectors within the traditional political system is demonstrated by governmental indifference toward such projects as low-cost housing and expanded public utilities in poorer urban neighborhoods, by selective enforcement of what often appears to be quite progressive social legislation, and by severe sanctions for those who would promote the alleviation of their grievances through strikes, demonstrations, and the occupation of factories. In short, when mobilized individuals become aware of new needs and the inability or unwillingness of traditional political structures to accept their participation and demands as legitimate, the time is propitious for the development of populist political movements.[22]

CHAPTER 2

POPULIST CHALLENGE AND

LIBERAL RESPONSE

In the 1960s, Thomas McGann's *Argentina: A Divided Land* was the most popular English-language introduction to Argentine politics. As the title suggests, McGann's study was an analysis of the nation's profound social, economic, geographic, and political cleavages. The popularity of this slim volume reflected in part the prevailing view among North Americans that Argentina lacked nothing but unity of national purpose. Unable to reach a consensus on the appropriate role of various political and economic forces, including those classic market forces that seemed to dictate Argentina's role in the international economy, the Argentine people had lost their ability to mobilize the nation's abundant human and natural resources to produce a stable, progressive society. According to this view, the Argentines were mired in incessant squabbling over the distribution of power and privilege, thus squandering the opportunities that had once made them an object of envy among citizens of less favorably endowed Latin American countries.

In many ways the logic of McGann's analysis is more compelling today than it was two decades ago. Argentina's population is as homogeneous as any in Latin American save Uruguay; it is literate (94 percent), relatively wealthy ($2,230 GNP per capita), and well fed (a daily calorie supply per capita of 126 percent of minimum requirements). Disparities in the distribution of income are considerable but not significantly different from those found in Italy, the United States, or West Germany.[1] Although lacking in some respects, Argentina's endowment of natural resources includes the wondrous Pampa and near self-sufficiency in petroleum, two features of almost incalculable benefit in a world of chronic food and energy shortages.

Yet juxtaposed with these favorable features is a political system noted for its instability and violence. Excluding Bolivia, no Latin American nation can match Argentina's record in overthrowing constitutional governments. In the twenty-seven-year period from 1955 to mid-1982, Argentina had no fewer than twenty chief executives; the average tenure in office was eighteen months. Nine of these men (Lonardi [1955], Aramburu [1955], Guido [1962], Onganía [1966], Levingston [1970], Lanusse [1971], Videla [1976], Galtieri [1981], and Bignone [1982]) achieved power through military coups, and four ousted popularly elected governments. This number only includes those coups that were successful; the world is still awaiting research on the number of abortive attempts to replace an existing government in Argentina.

And few South American nations can match Argentina's recent record of human rights violations. The Argentine government and its paramilitary allies in the late 1970s refined the art of "disappearing" people to such an extent that in 1980 the founder of Argentina's Service for Justice and Peace, Adolfo Pérez Esquivel, received the Nobel peace prize for his defense of human rights against governmental terror.[2]

One goal of this volume is to explain why Argentines have failed to produce a stable, democratic political system. Before attacking that question, however, it is important to suggest that the "failure" of Argentina is at least in part in the eye of the beholder rather than in the Argentine social system. Armed with an arsenal of preconceptions regarding the appropriate forms of social organization for advanced Latin American societies, we in the United States in particular have tended to view as pathological any major deviations from our culture-bound expectations. It can be argued that there is a broad international consensus on the desirability of democracy over authoritarianism, but there is little agreement on the precise meaning of the term and even less agreement on the optimal way to move from the latter to the former. Given these disagreements (alongside the humbling evidence that we are able to convince little more than half of our eligible voters to go to the polls once every four years), it may be that our expectations regarding democracy in Argentina are unfulfilled because our expectations are unreasonable, based upon values that simply lack relevance in Argentina and that may, moreover, lack relevance in discussions of democracy. To paraphrase Claudio Véliz, political change in Argentina is unlikely to be understood by those who insist on considering Argentina as an incipient Western European country or an overdeveloped part of the Third World.[3] Despite the expectations encouraged by extraneous political beliefs, Argentina has been clearly unresponsive to attempts to impose reforms that ignore the nation's history. It is improbable that this will change very much in the foreseeable future.

Expectations and perceptions aside, the basic argument presented in this book is that political conflict in contemporary Argentina is rooted in an unresolved—and perhaps unresolvable—conflict between two strongly opposed views of the appropriate social structure for Argentina, often expressed as a conflict between two rival economic policies: the *liberalism* of the British Manchester School variety versus what Richard Mallon and Juan Sourrouille have called *national populism*.[4] Here in the economic realm the conflict stands out in sharpest relief: liberals advocate an economic system open and responsive to international influences, while national populists argue for policies that favor native entrepreneurs and a relatively high level of economic autonomy.

Much more will be said below about the economic basis of political conflict in contemporary Argentina; what must be emphasized at the outset, however, is that this cleavage is much more than a technical disagreement over the appropriate policies to foster a stable, progressive economy. As it has for the past four decades, Argentina today lacks a basic consensus on the type of society Argentines should attempt to construct. Absent this agreement, the nation has lurched uncertainly through most of the twentieth century, and it will undoubtedly continue to do so until it reaches a consensus on goals that are both economically feasible and politically acceptable to a broad segment of the Argentine people.

As of this writing, in late 1982, the liberal approach has once again provided Argentina with a period of extraordinarily inept leadership. The present regime has not only resorted to gross violations of fundamental human rights but has also accomplished the destruction of the Argentine economy *and* the military humiliation of the Argentine people in the ill-advised, ill-conceived, and ill-executed adventure to retake the Malvinas. Meanwhile, there is clear evidence that the populist view has commanded the loyalty of the majority of Argentine citizens since perhaps the turn of the century and certainly since World War II. It is possible to argue that the liberal perspective is now moribund and that any workable consensus in Argentine politics will have to tilt heavily in favor of the policies and structures favored by populist political groups. That is the assumption of this volume: the focus upon the nature of mass support for Argentine populism reflects a belief that populism will eventually achieve a definitive victory over its liberal rivals. One must then wonder what types of policies will be pursued by the victor, what social groups populism will speak for, and how unified its voice will be. The postwar history of Peronism provides substantial clues that help to answer these questions, but to understand Peronism we must first examine the populist roots from which it sprung.

THE CHALLENGE OF NATIONAL POPULISM

Nearly half a century before the birth of Juan Perón in 1895, profound demographic and economic changes had begun to transform Argentine society. The blending of British capital with Spanish and Italian immigration, impressive technological innovations, and European demand for the products of the Pampa acted as solvents to loosen the hold of traditional social and political structures upon a people noted for their impatience with anachronisms. Later, the economic dislocations of the Depression, coupled with substantial internal migration, provided further impetus to social change. Out of these disruptive processes emerged a population distinct from that of previous generations. This was the alluvial period of Argentine history, when emerging social groups of indefinite characteristics fitfully created their positions in the Argentine political system. It was the period when contemporary sociopolitical cleavages were created.

In the fifty years prior to the onset of the 1929 Depression, the Argentine economy experienced a sustained period of growth unmatched in its economic history. Shortly after the fall of Juan Manuel de Rosas in 1852, a foreign-oriented boom of impressive proportions began to transform the nation into Europe's provisioner. Although essentially directed toward the production of rural commodities for export, the Argentine economy also increasingly supported the growth of domestic light industry; by 1895 there were over twenty-three thousand industrial establishments, catering primarily to the needs of individual consumers and the rapidly growing number of exporters. While Argentina possessed no official policy of industrialization before 1930, as early as 1906, taking note of both the desirability of industrial protection and the attractive size of potential customs revenues, the government reenacted relatively stiff tariffs, which further stimulated local entrepreneurs.[5] Nevertheless, compared to the Pampa's impressive agricultural bounty, Argentine industrial production was meager until the 1930s, and, significantly, booms in the latter were invariably predicated upon cyclical upswings in the former.[6]

The crash of the 1930s demonstrated as never before the fragile, dependent nature of Argentina's economy. A severely curtailed capacity to import and an equally catastrophic export market forced Argentine policymakers to adopt a number of innovative measures that redounded to the benefit of domestic industrial production. Quantitative restrictions on imports, higher tariffs, and immensely important multiple exchange rates stimulated import-substituting industry.[7] Facing this seemingly inexorable disappearance of one of His Majesty's most lucrative foreign markets, Britain's commercial attaché informed his London superiors from Buenos Aires in 1935 that "the general increase in tariffs which took place in 1931 and the even more considerable protection granted by the sudden devaluation of the Argentine peso toward the end of 1933 stimulated the local industrial manufacture of a large quantity of products which previously had been imported. . . . Such measures more than adequately counterbalance the 1933 reductions in tariff levies obtained for certain goods produced in the United Kingdom."[8] During the great export boom of the 1925–29 quinquennium, rural production accounted for nearly twice as much of the Argentine gross national product as did the nation's nascent industrial sector. Between 1936 and 1946 the number of industrial facilities doubled, however, and midway through this decade an era ended as industry's contribution to Argentina's GNP finally surpassed that of agriculture.[9]

The expansion of the labor force which accompanied this flourishing industrial production was equally impressive. By 1947 fully three-quarters of the economically active population was engaged in secondary- or tertiary-sector pursuits, and the number of industrial establishments employing five hundred or more blue-collar workers (*obreros*) skyrocketed to 331, a leap of 372 percent between 1935 and 1947.[10] During this same period blue-collar employment in industry rose no less than 124 percent, nearly all of the increase taking place before the end of World War II.

Many of these new workers came over in the massive wave of European immigration that flooded Argentina from about 1870 until the beginning of World War I (see Table 2.1). The number of foreign immigrants was large—they accounted for 30 percent of the Argentine population in 1914—but their interest in political activity appears to have been checked by the very low feelings of political efficacy that formed part of the cognitive baggage that predominantly lower-class immigrants brought to the New World from Southern Europe. Except in certain municipal elections, only citizens could vote and only voters could hold office, and in 1914 less

TABLE 2.1

Argentina's Foreign-Born Population: Males Twenty Years Old and Over

	Buenos Aires		Selected Provinces[a]	
	Citizens	Noncitizens	Citizens	Noncitizens
1869	12,000	48,000	—	—
1895	42,000	174,000	287,000	309,000
1914	119,000	404,000	557,000	752,000
1947	614,000	433,000	2,115,000	747,000

Source: Gino Germani, "Mass Immigration and Modernization in Argentina,"
p. 173.
a. Includes the provinces of Buenos Aires, Córdoba, Entre Ríos, Mendoza, and
La Pampa.

than 1 percent of Argentina's immigrants had bothered to comply
with the nation's relatively moderate naturalization laws.[11] By 1947
the number had risen to 7 percent. Despite these figures, it is
appropriate to emphasize the existence of this new population, for
voting is not the only or even the most prominent form of political
participation in Argentina.

Of far greater political consequence in the 1940s was the concen-
tration of Argentina's population (see Table 2.2). With less than
1 percent of the nation's territory, the Argentine littoral accommo-
dated 26 percent of the population in 1914. By 1944 fully 57 percent
of all Argentines resided in either the Federal Capital or the provinces of Buenos Aires and Santa Fe. By 1947 nearly 69 percent of all
blue-collar workers produced three-quarters of the nation's industrial goods within the boundaries of the Federal Capital and the
province of Buenos Aires.[12]

Despite spurts before and after World War II, European immigration slowed considerably following World War I. Since Argentina
has long maintained a birthrate among the lowest in the hemi-
sphere, the burgeoning post-World War I urban growth resulted
from substantial migration from the rural areas and lesser amounts
of immigration from neighboring Chile, Bolivia, and Paraguay. In
the early 1940s the Ortiz and Castillo governments were quick to
recognize the potentially deleterious economic effects of rural de-

TABLE 2.2

Urban-Rural Population Distributions, 1947

Area	Percentage Urban	Percentage Rural	Percentage of Total Urban Population
Greater Buenos Aires	98.8	1.2	45.9
Littoral	53.8	46.2	38.7
Northwest	38.1	61.9	6.9
Center and West	47.4	52.6	4.8
Northeast	25.5	74.5	2.1
South	31.0	69.0	1.6
Total	62.0	38.0	100.0

Source: Gino Germani, *Estructura social de la Argentina*, p. 72.

population, and study groups were commissioned to devise means of reversing the flow.

These managed only to assemble a statistical description of the phenomenon and to offer a number of alternative explanations for its ubiquity. Among these were such "push" incentives as the exhaustion of productive farmlands, droughts and plant diseases, and increased rural unemployment resulting from mechanization as well as such "pull" incentives as higher urban wages and an enticing urban social ambience.[13] The intensity of the phenomenon was also signaled: in the province of Buenos Aires half of the one hundred counties were becoming depopulated—8 percent gravely, 12 percent gradually, and 30 percent in the initial stages in 1946. Although such major urban areas as Rosario, Paraná, Córdoba, and Mendoza received substantial numbers of rural migrants, their principal destination was Greater Buenos Aires.

More important, this migration process began in earnest sometime after 1936, for in that year only 12 percent of the 3.4 million inhabitants of Greater Buenos Aires had been born elsewhere in Argentina.[14] Soon thereafter, what Germani terms a "rain of migrants" began to flood into Buenos Aires. It has been variously estimated that during the peak years between 1943 and 1947 somewhere between 117,000 and 142,000 migrants arrived each year in the capital's urban complex, figures which represent at least

40 percent of the interior's net population growth.[15] By 1947, therefore, 37 percent of the city's population of 4.7 million had been born elsewhere in Argentina. For the nation as a whole, in 1947, 25 percent of all citizens were living in provinces other than those of their birth, and more than three-fourths of this number had congregated in the Argentine littoral.[16]

All of these economic and demographic changes profoundly influenced Argentine politics long before Perón's rise to power. They caused two pre-Perón political developments that are of crucial importance to an understanding of contemporary Argentina: the definitive electoral defeat of liberalism by national populists and the rise of working-class political consciousness.

The Electoral Defeat of Liberalism

The roots of national populism are not difficult to determine: they are closely linked with, if not inseparable from, the founding of the Únión Cívica in 1890. Prior to that date Argentina's political party structure was typical of nineteenth-century Latin America. First there were conservatives and democrats, then federalists and unitarians, and, after the fall of Rosas in 1852, liberals and federalists. In 1861 Mitre's victory over Urquiza's federalists in the Battle of Pavón gave the Buenos Aires liberals firm control of Argentina's political system. Although the liberals were to split and splinter several times (into nationalists, autonomists, republicans, national autonomists), they never lost their grip on politics during the balance of the nineteenth century. By the time Miguel Juárez Celman succeeded Julio A. Roca in 1886, the Partido Autonomista Nacional (PAN) had become the only visible party in the country, and Juárez's administration was appropriately dubbed the *unicato*. The "únicos" were primarily the nation's landowners. According to José Ingenieros, "Argentine politics during the nineteenth century had been the monopoly of one social class—the landowners—at whose side lived crowds of mestizos that were neither a middle class nor a proletariat."[17]

It was about the time of the *unicato* that the socioeconomic changes discussed above began to have a noticeable effect on politics. In April 1890 the Unión Cívica (UC) was formed to contest the political monopoly of the *estancieros* and exporters. The heirs to this movement have become so mild in their political activity that it is easy to forget that the UC was initially a radical organization, accusing the government of "ineptitude and immorality in public ad-ministration, suppression of free suffrage, and moral decadence."[18] In fact, three months after the party's formation the middle- and upper-class leadership issued a call to revolution: "The directors of the Civic Union, convinced of the absolute impossibility of ob-taining by peaceful means political reform that the honor and wel-fare of the nation demand, solemnly resolve a supreme and very sad sacrifice: revolution."[19] The revolt was short-lived, but it re-sulted in President Juárez Celman's resignation. The era of growth had begun for the Unión Cívica.

The strength of the Unión Cívica Radical (UCR—the UC split in 1891 into the UCR and the Unión Cívica Principista over the issue of an accord with the PAN) lay in its growing middle-class base: urban merchants, clerks, and professionals plus small landowners of the littoral, especially Santa Fe, landowners who lacked a political party prior to the formation of the UCR. The party's principal goal was free, competitive elections as a mechanism to achieve popular sovereignty. After party leaders Leandro Alem committed suicide and Aristóbulo del Valle died of natural causes in 1896, leadership fell to younger men, particularly Hipólito Yrigoyen. He led the fledgling party into a period of internal division and a policy of nonparticipation in the liberals' electoral fraud. Slowly, the UCR developed into a mature party.

The election of liberal Roque Sáenz Peña in 1910 signaled the liberals' agreement to share power with the UCR. The motivating factor behind this generosity was probably a perception among liberal elites that a considerable portion of the population viewed their hold on power as illegitimate. During the *unicato* the opposi-tion was either nonexistent or not mobilized; after the founding of the UCR, the opposition was both evident and intransigent. Thus Sáenz Peña offered the UCR several cabinet positions, only to be rebuffed by Yrigoyen: "Our determination not to participate in the government is immutable; the only thing that could change our resolution is honorable elections guaranteed by electoral reform."[20]

And so there was electoral reform. The Sáenz Peña Law (passed in three sections in 1911–12) provided for secret, obligatory, and universal male suffrage. In the subsequent election of 1916, Hipó-lito Yrigoyen was elected president by an overwhelming margin: 51 percent of the popular vote with the remainder split among three candidates, the most popular of whom received 21 percent of the popular vote. With this election, Argentina's liberals were forced to surrender public office, and since then liberals have never again been able to gain control of the central government except through military coups.

After the advent of Peronism it became common to deprecate the work of early UCR administrations, to assert that apart from its rhetoric the UCR differed but little from its liberal predecessors.[21] This is probably an incorrect assessment. The UCR successfully implemented a large number of major reform programs in the areas of education, public health, and workers' rights. All of these proposals were opposed by the liberals, who also objected strenuously to the UCR's efforts to bring the state into areas of the economy previously reserved for the private sector. In 1919, Yrigoyen issued an executive decree nationalizing all petroleum deposits, and three years later he founded the state oil company, YPF, which to Argentine nationalists has always been a symbol of defiance of foreign domination of national resources.[22] In 1920, Yrigoyen gave his party's view of the role of the state in the economy: "The state ought to acquire a preponderant position in the industrial activities of the nation in order to respond to the need for services, and in some areas these activities ought to be substituted for the application of private capital; in nations of constant and progressive development such as ours, public services should be considered as principally the instrument of government."[23] This was a substantial innovation in Argentine political history.

Thus, while it is true that the UCR has never represented a coherent political viewpoint, and equally true that its period in power (1916–30) was characterized by indecisiveness, it is not correct to conclude that no significant policy changes occurred under UCR administrations. Furthermore, it is a mistake to focus only upon concrete policy changes in order to assess the UCR's contribution to contemporary Argentine politics, for the party also contributed an *attitude* to Argentine politics. In its moment on the political stage, the UCR solidified the position of popular sovereignty as the arbitrator of national political struggles. Thus, in his farewell address to the Argentine people in 1973, General Alejandro Lanusse felt obliged to thank his fellow citizens for their patience with a government that had not been elected. That Lanusse felt such an obligation is a direct result of the contributions of the UCR. While the party is now moribund, before it lapsed into semiconsciousness it created an entirely new attitude toward popular sovereignty, an attitude that is, after all, the cornerstone of populism.

The Political Mobilization of the Working Class

Writers who consider Juan Perón an aberration on an otherwise "normal" political landscape have often explained the success of Peronism by its leader's demagogic ability to create a *new* consciousness among Argentina's rapidly expanding urban working class. Such an interpretation is more than incorrect; by implication it also promotes the belief that the extirpation of Perón and Peronism will lead to the decline of populism and a return to the liberal-oriented era of social peace in Argentina.

The development of a political consciousness among members of the Argentine working class was well advanced years before the 1943 coup that ousted President Castillo, but little effort had been made to integrate these marginal groups into Argentina's political system. As Peter Smith has demonstrated,

> in the late nineteen-thirties and early forties leaders . . .
> sought to promote urban mass interests through established
> and constitutional political institutions. Before 1943 these
> leaders, mostly Socialists, were stopped at every turn by the
> ruling Concordancia; and the institutions through which they
> pressed their demands, particularly the national Congress,
> were devitalized and discredited. The critical point is that
> socially mobilized groups sought political participation, but
> were not given access to power. The inevitable result was
> frustration. Perón's entrance on to the scene came, then, at a
> propitious time.[24]

There are at least two plausible reasons why spokesmen for the working class were unsuccessful. The first is that no party or interest association had yet been formed which mobilized workers felt inclined to support: that is, the spokesmen spoke for themselves and perhaps a small following, but not for the working class. The second is that such an association did exist and did attract broad worker support, but traditional political actors were so entrenched in power that for the time being their defeat proved impossible.

The first alternative seems improbable when the actual vote is inspected, for in the Federal Capital the Socialist party ran second to the UCR in 1940 and *first* in 1942. Moreover, there is a clear relationship between social class and electoral behavior in these two elections. The correlations between occupation and the vote for eight parties in the 1942 Federal Capital election of national deputies indicate that strong conservative voting patterns were restricted to areas with high percentages of professionals and university students (see Table 2.3). Since the Partido Conservador received less than 1 percent of the vote and the Unión de Contribuyentes scarcely fared better, the conservative vote is best indicated by results for the Lista de Concordancia, literally a list of candidates put forward by the semiinstitutionalized coalition of right and center-right parties which ruled Argentina throughout the 1930s. With over 21 percent of the popular vote, the Concordancia presumably provided conservative electors with an acceptable alternative to the centrist UCR and the three labor-oriented parties. Most important, the correlation coefficients in Table 2.3 suggest that these votes represent social-class preferences.

The same cannot be said of the vote for the UCR, for although 29 percent of the electorate selected this option, no particular social group supplied a disproportionate share of the total Radical electoral strength. But the vote for the two principal labor-oriented parties, the Socialists and the Concentración Obrera, exhibits rather strong social-class relationships. Since the latter received slightly less than 8 percent of the popular vote, much greater attention should be accorded the Partido Socialista (PS), which actually won the election with one-third of all votes cast. The correlations in Table 2.3 suggest a linkage between lower social class and voting for the labor-oriented Socialists, but the fact that they are not terribly high probably indicates the depressing influence of additional support from other social groups. The coefficients can be depressed either because the Socialists did not attract enough of the labor vote or because they attracted some of the middle-class and upper-class vote as well. Since the PS outpolled all its opponents, the latter interpretation seems more appropriate. The most logical inference is not that the working class failed to identify a party to articulate its goals and grievances but rather that it had to share its party with other Argentines.

This extremely important point is substantiated by collapsing the vote for eight parties into three categories: labor, center, and right. The coefficients in Table 2.4 indicate a clear relationship between upper-class conservatism and working-class laborism. The preference for centrist parties does continue to exhibit a relatively unbiased, multiclass nature, but the data suggest that there is simply no justification for the assertion that class-conscious voting patterns first emerged with the initial Peronist election in 1946. The apparent conclusion is that the mobilized working class did indeed perceive the Socialist party as its champion. Thus the first ex-

TABLE 2.3

Correlations between Occupation and Party Vote, Federal Capital, 1942

(N=209 *circuitos*)

Occupation	PS	Concentración Obrera	Socialista Obrera	UCR	Radical	Unión de Contribuyentes	Concordancia	Conservador
Professionals	−.39	−.36	−.20	−.20	−.02	.53	.55	.00
Students	−.36	−.39	−.29	−.10	.00	.49	.50	−.08
Businessmen	.11	−.12	−.20	−.04	−.08	.17	.00	.00
White-collar employees	.13	−.08	.06	.13	.04	.19	−.21	.05
Blue-collar workers	.29	.49	.15	.02	.03	−.62	−.39	−.08
Unskilled workers	−.03	.21	.13	.02	.00	−.14	−.17	−.14
Percent of total vote	33.1	7.5	4.1	28.9	2.5	1.8	21.4	0.7

Source: Secretaría Electoral de la Capital Federal.

TABLE 2.4

Correlations between Occupation and Party Vote, Federal Capital, 1942

(N=209 *circuitos*)

Occupation	Party Orientation		
	Labor[a]	Center[b]	Conservative[c]
Professionals	−.49	−.14	.58
Students	−.49	−.05	.52
Businessmen	.04	−.06	.01
White-collar employees	.09	.17	−.21
Blue-collar workers	.45	−.04	−.43
Unskilled workers	.07	.01	−.08

Source: Secretaría Electoral de la Capital Federal.
a. Labor: Concentración Obrera, Partido Socialista Obrero, Partido Socialista.
b. Center: Partido Radical, Unión Cívica Radical.
c. Conservative: Partido Conservador, Lista de Concordancia, Unión de Contribuyentes.

planatory alternative—that no party existed to represent mobilized lower-class Argentines—seems untenable.

Although it is difficult to overlook the Socialists' consistently strong prolabor position, there has long existed a tendency to deprecate the extent of the party's commitment to the alleviation of working-class grievances.[25] The fact that it adopted a parliamentary approach to reform and eschewed violent revolution should no more disqualify the PS as the spokesman for the working class in Argentina than it would the Labour party in Britain. Nor should the Socialists' middle-class intellectual leadership be interpreted as an obstacle to the attraction of lower-class supporters, for intellectuals have made up at least part of the leadership in every major working-class party in the world. Finally, once Perón had captured the allegiance of the urban working class, the party that had won the 1942 Federal Capital election was left four years later without a single representative in Congress for the first time since 1912. This is a strong indication of the source of the earlier Socialist strength.

Thus it is probable that the inability of the working class to demonstrate significant political power prior to 1943 reflected the unassailable position of Argentina's traditional political actors. Eventually, of course, more and larger concessions would have to be made to a mobilized, expanding urban working class, but for the time being the working class could be continually stymied by the imposing political and economic power of the antagonistic influences colloquially referred to as the oligarchy. Perón did what the Socialists could not do because he had all the guns, and Perón won their constituency because he could deliver what the Socialists would have delivered had they enjoyed his monopoly on force. It is not unreasonable to conclude that the Socialists were defeated because they patiently pursued these same goals within the framework of Argentina's constitution. This strategy cannot be dismissed as the creation of utopian intellectuals lacking a comprehension of workers' goals and frustrations; rather it sprung from hardened politicians who had demonstrated their skill and understanding in 1942 by defeating the entrenched liberals *and* the rival national populists—the UCR—in Argentina's most important electoral district.

THE POSTWAR POPULIST COALITION

Since the mid-1940s, primary responsibility for carrying the banner of Argentine populism has rested with the Peronists, a heterogeneous coalition of a variety of social groups: the part of the armed forces that is committed to industrialization as a projection of national power, the nonentrepreneurial white-collar work force, part of the national bourgeoisie, and, of course, the working class.[26] As Table 2.5 indicates, since 1946 this coalition has consistently maintained at least an electoral plurality, and on several occasions it has received a simple majority—a remarkable achievement in the multiparty environment of Argentine politics.

Over the past thirty-five years, some coalition members have abandoned the Peronists, but most of them have regularly returned to the coalition when the available alternatives were perceived as less attractive. Thus Peronism has been broadly inclusive, excluding only those groups that have refused to pursue a path of conciliation and compromise. Primary among these are, first, the diehard liberals who reject populist economic policies and, second, the limited number of organizations that insist upon a revolutionary, exclusionary view of political participation.

Given the nature of Argentina's national populist coalition, one of the most confusing aspects of Peronism has always been its view of the role of explicit class conflict in fostering social change. Pe-

TABLE 2.5

Argentine Election Results, 1946–1973 (percentages)

	1946	1951	1957[a]	1960	1962	1965	1973
Peronista	52.4	62.5	24.3	24.9	31.9	34.5	61.9
Unión Democrática	42.5						
Unión Cívica Radical		31.8					24.4
Unión Cívica Radical Popular			24.2	23.7	24.5	28.6	
Unión Cívica Radical Intransigente (UCRI)			21.2	20.6	19.9	4.4	
Movimiento de Integración y Desarrollo						6.3	
Demócrata Cristiano			4.8	3.9	2.3	2.6	
Socialista		0.7	6.0	8.4	4.5	3.8	1.6
Other parties	5.1	5.0	19.5	18.5	16.9	19.8	12.1
Total	100.	100.	100.	100.	100.	100.	100.

Source: Peter G. Snow, *Argentine Political Parties and the 1966 Revolution*, p. 50; Ministerio del Interior, Dirección Nacional Electoral.

a. In 1957 many Peronists disobeyed Perón and voted for the UCRI.

Note: Only the 1946 and 1973 elections were for the presidency. The elections of 1951, 1960, and 1962 were all congressional elections. The 1957 election was to select delegates to a constitutional convention. There were two presidential elections in 1973; the data here are from the September contest.

rón's words might have clarified his movement's understanding of class struggle were it not for the unfortunate fact that *El líder* always displayed the annoying habit of cultivating his audience's predispositions. Speaking at a luncheon for stockbrokers, he said, "I do not believe that the solutions to social problems are in continuing the struggle between capital and labor."[27] Philosophizing for posterity, he stated: "Society is not now a grouping of opposed forces but a harmonizing of them, that is, now men are not enemies of other men but rather they constitute a reconciled and happy community. . . . The creations of mankind are not constructed by separation and hate, but with collaboration and love."[28] To a rally for garment workers, he said, "Eva Perón always said that the class struggle only ends with the elimination of one of the classes."[29]

Despite frequent comments to the contrary at union-organized demonstrations, it now appears certain that one of Perón's principal preoccupations was the conciliation of Argentina's social classes. "I believe that the social problem solves itself in but one way: working conscientiously to look for a perfect regulation among the working, middle, and capitalist classes, procuring a perfect harmony of forces. . . . Wealth without social stability can be powerful, but it will always be fragile, and that is the danger . . . the Secretariat of Labor and Welfare tries to avoid by all means."[30] Just as he had championed labor organization because "an inorganic working mass is a breeding ground for the most foreign political and ideological concepts," Perón promoted class harmony through social justice as a deterrent to political unrest. "We could not have demanded of our population greater sacrifice without offering a greater well-being, because our working masses were fed by the marxist doctrine and directed by leaders with clearly marxist inspiration. If we had demanded it we would have precipitated a social revolution."[31] Perón, in short, was concerned that unorganized workers could exacerbate societal conflicts to the point of revolution. Thus the Peronist approach was to structure the lower class and preclude its independence while simultaneously providing social justice to alleviate its most pressing grievances. Firmly convinced that a society's institutions "cannot be broken without negative disequilibriums," state-directed class conciliation became the Justicialist answer to the increasingly popular alternative of violent social upheaval.[32]

A coalition predicated upon class conciliation is viable only so long as social and economic conditions permit the simultaneous gratification of demands by different classes or groups. In practice, this means that rapid economic growth is essential, for redistributive policies in a time of scarcity would inevitably alienate some part of an inclusionary coalition. During periods of economic stagnation, any multiclass coalition, such as Peronism, will quickly fragment, as the individual groups contest for severely limited rewards.[33] To understand how the processes of growth and stagnation have affected contemporary Argentine politics, it is necessary first to concentrate upon the nature of working-class and urban-middle-class support for Peronism and then to examine the means by which Perón fabricated his national populist coalition.

Social Class and Electoral Support for Peronism

The social-class orientation of Argentine politics is demonstrated most dramatically by the correlations between occupation and candidate preference in 1946, the year Perón was first elected president of Argentina. In Table 2.6 the correlations between occupation and the vote for Perón indicate the existence of a tendency toward upper-class and working-class electoral polarization.[34] This is common knowledge, of course, and needs little emphasis here. The correlations between occupation and the Peronist vote in the 209 precincts of the Federal Capital between 1946 and 1973 are presented in Table 2.7; Table 2.8 contains similar data for the 39 wards and counties of Greater Buenos Aires. While the use of these aggregate electoral data and broad occupational categories might obscure fine distinctions and overemphasize the unidirectionality of upper-class and working-class electoral behavior, it remains apparent that areas of relatively large working-class social composition are those which strongly support the Peronist movement.

These data linking the working class to Peronism were confirmed by Jeane Kirkpatrick's 1965 survey analysis.[35] While she emphasized that Peronism is not a single-class movement, Kirkpatrick did find that the Peronists are disproportionately associated with the Argentine working class (see Table 2.9). And, significantly, she also found that these "lower-class Peronists demonstrated a class consciousness unique among Argentines."[36]

The insignificant values registered by white-collar employees in the Federal Capital (Table 2.7) contradict similar data from Greater Buenos Aires (Table 2.8) and occasional assertions that the Argentine middle class was and remains vehemently anti-Peronist. Juan José Sebreli's influential work, for example, characterizes Peronism as "a challenge to petit bourgeois traditions, customs,

TABLE 2.6

*Social Class: Pearson Correlations between
Occupation and the Peronist Vote,
Federal Capital, 1946* (N=209)

Occupation	Perón–Quijano[a]
% Professionals	−.70
% Students	−.67
% Businessmen	−.41
% White-collar employees	−.04
% Blue-collar workers	.79
% Unskilled workers	.24

Source: Secretaría Electoral de la Capital Federal.
a. Endorsed by the Partido Laborista, UCR–Junta
Renovadora, Juventud Renovadora Argentina, and the
Partido Patriótico 4 de Junio.

established values, moral clichés, Philistine inhibitions, and hypo-critical ideology of virtue. . . . The middle class reacted to this his-torical process which it did not understand with an hysterical anti-Peronism."[37] Recent empirical studies, however, cast doubt upon Sebreli's interpretation and the negative correlations in Table 2.8. The more reliable data from the Federal Capital's 209 precincts (Table 2.7) produce directionless correlation coefficients. In addi-tion, Kirkpatrick's survey discerned a tendency for the Peronist movement to attract a substantial middle-class following: "Middle-income respondents are well represented among Peronists, com-prising approximately one-third of the persons who supported Perón for President and a larger portion of those with sympathy for the movement."[38] Both Kirkpatrick's analysis and the data in Table 2.7 suggest that very little faith should be placed in Sebreli's im-pressions or in the reliability of the middle-class coefficients in Table 2.8.

The Argentine Working Class

While there is intense disagreement over Perón's character, there has never been much dispute over his political acumen. He was an uncommonly astute politician, and it was primarily when certain character deficiencies (avarice, vanity, licentiousness) were allowed

TABLE 2.7

Social Class: Pearson Correlations between
Occupation and the Peronist Vote,
Federal Capital, 1946–1973 (N=209)

Occupation	PERON[a]	1946	1951	1957	1960	1962	1965	1973
% Professionals	-.71	-.70	-.66	-.61	-.67	-.66	-.65	-.71
% Students	-.72	-.67	-.68	-.63	-.69	-.64	-.69	-.71
% Businessmen	-.47	-.41	-.39	-.44	-.43	-.44	-.49	-.45
% White-collar employees	-.05	-.04	-.11	-.12	-.05	.01	-.06	.04
% Blue-collar workers	.81	.79	.80	.70	.76	.71	.74	.70
% Unskilled workers	.33	.24	.26	.33	.33	.28	.35	.34

Source: Secretaría Electoral de la Capital Federal.
a. PERON is a composite variable representing the sum of the products of each election's standardized score and its factor score coefficient (see appendix).

TABLE 2.8

Social Class: Pearson Correlations between
Occupation and the Peronist Vote,
Greater Buenos Aires, 1946–1973 (N=39)

Occupation	PERON 1946	1954	1957	1960	1962	1965	1973
% Professionals, 1960	−.96	−.83	−.95	−.90	−.89	−.94	−.84	−.96
% Students, 1960	−.80	−.60	−.80	−.71	−.75	−.81	−.72	−.86
% White-collar employees, 1960	−.72	−.47	−.74	−.68	−.73	−.74	−.64	−.77
% Blue-collar workers, 1960	.91	.76	.91	.88	.88	.92	.80	.90

Source: Ministerio del Interior, Dirección Nacional Electoral; Dirección Nacional de Estadística y Censos, *Censo nacional de población 1960.*

TABLE 2.9

Socioeconomic Characteristics and Orientations toward Peronism, 1965

	Percentage of Class[a]		
	Lower (N=721)	Middle (N=960)	Upper (N=157)
Would vote for Perón	32.0	13.0	6.4
Generally approve of Peronist movement	38.7	18.4	12.7
Would support candidate supporting Perón	32.6	15.2	7.0
Perón did most to harm Argentina	19.4	39.5	65.0
Would hurt Argentina for Perón to return	34.8	56.7	77.7

Source: Kirkpatrick, *Leader and Vanguard in Mass Society*, p. 97.
a. Class characterization based on interviewer appraisal.

to override political intuition that his movement foundered. One product of this astute judgment was an appreciation of the latent power of the Argentine working class. One of Perón's assistants in the Secretariat of Labor and Welfare in 1943 was a capable Spanish bureaucrat, José Figuerola, whose tasks included the gathering and analysis of demographic data. These data indicated to Perón (but not, apparently, to the UCR) that the future of national populism rested in large measure with the urban working class. As Table 2.10 suggests, in the mid-1940s at least 40 percent of all Argentines were engaged in urban-working-class economic activity, a figure which jumps to 63 percent if both the lower and lower-middle secondary and tertiary workers are combined. The question for Perón was how the latent political power of the Argentine working class could be made manifest. His answer made him the most important man in Argentine history.

If Perón's success can be attributed to the political participation of Argentina's working class, it is equally true that the strength of the Argentine labor movement can be attributed to the Peronist governments.[39] The very active political role that this symbiotic relationship implies for the forces of organized labor is often misinterpreted by observers in the United States accustomed to unions

TABLE 2.10

Argentine Social Class Structure by Economic Sector, 1947
(percentages)

Economic Sector

Class	Primary	Secondary	Tertiary	Other	Total
Upper	0.3	0.1	0.3	0.0	0.7
Upper middle	1.1	1.5	3.8	0.2	6.6
Lower middle	8.2	4.4	17.1	3.2	32.9
Lower	16.0	21.9	19.5	2.4	59.8
Total	25.6	27.8	40.5	6.1	100.0

Source: Germani, *Estructura social de la Argentina,* pp. 196–97.

ostensibly dedicated primarily to labor-management relations and theoretically free from partisan political conflict. This ideal type is rarely to be found, however, and least of all in Argentina, where, as Peter Snow says, "the leader of a large union . . . is almost automatically a prominent national politician; the Secretary General of the General Confederation of Labor holds potential political power which is probably equal to that of the leader of a major political party."[40] Perhaps, as Roberto Carri has stated, Argentina's highly politicized labor organizations are a result of Perón's failure to organize a coherent political party, a failure that forced him to turn to organized labor.[41] For whatever reason, though, the majority factions of the nation's labor movement have long acted as a surrogate Peronist political party, particularly during those years when veiled and outright proscriptions have precluded a traditional party organization. The Confederación General del Trabajo (CGT) and its constituent unions function, in turn, as the principal vehicles for working-class political participation in Argentina.

The policy of Argentina's liberal governments toward organized labor can best be described as one of hostile neglect. Prior to the first Peronist administration there had been a National Department of Labor, but it had suffered an illustratively inauspicious initiation: it was created by decree rather than law in 1907 when the Senate refused to fund its first year of operation. Not until 1912 did Congress provide the department with a *ley orgánica* to outline its functions and composition, and then it was awarded jurisdiction only in the Federal Capital and national territories, leaving the fourteen provinces to decide whether to establish similar autonomous organizations.[42] Decades later this provision for autonomy would lead to a constitutional crisis and, eventually, to Perón's famous purge of the Supreme Court.[43]

In practice, the department became sedentary, serving merely as a source of labor statistics. But other government agencies actively participated in the field of labor relations. As Ernesto Sábato indicates, the police became closely linked to antiunion activity in the first decades of the twentieth century.

> They were spoken to about Liberty, but jailed when they went out on strike; they were spoken to about Justice, but were locked up without due process and barbarously tortured in the Special Section against Communism, and *habeas corpus* and other resources in a theoretically existent system of justice were ridiculed with brutal cynicism in regular practice; they were spoken to about the Fatherland, but the public powers defended the English or North American packing houses.[44]

Prior to Perón, labor-management relations were governed by the law of supply and demand, with direct employee-employer bargaining bypassing the department on almost all occasions and not infrequently the employees' union as well.[45] Labor's principal participation in national politics was at the end of a policeman's club.

The movement's perpetual state of internal anarchy plagued union organizational efforts long before it drove Perón to distraction. The CGT, which had been founded only in 1936 by a consolidation of the Confederación Obrera Argentina and the Unión Sindical Argentina (USA), had split once more in late 1942 following a bitter struggle for the organization's secretary-generalship. Earlier, a splinter of the USA had reformed as a separate federation, whose relatively negligible strength rested in the maritime workers and Luis Gay's telephone employees. Finally, although its only strong affiliate (the Federación Obrera Local Bonaerense) had been closed by the government since 1932, the anarchist Federación Obrera Regional Argentina (FORA) continued to harass employers, the government, and the CGT's efforts to consolidate the union movement. In the early 1940s FORA showed potential new strength by staging a protracted strike at the Firestone rubber plant.

Despite these divisions, by the time of the June 1943 revolution and the beginning of Perón's career in national politics, labor's limited strength remained concentrated in the two factions of the

CGT. The stronger of the two, the CGT No. 1, which was dominated by the two railroad unions (La Fraternidad and the Unión Ferroviaria), maintained a socialist orientation. Its secretary-general, José Domenech, also acted as secretary general of the Unión Ferroviaria. The CGT No. 2, led by the socialist chieftain of the municipal workers, Francisco Pérez Leiros, received its strength from the Communist-dominated construction, metallurgical, and textile unions, a fact the revolutionary government would use to justify dissolving the entire organization in July 1943. The commercial employees' (led by Perón's future interior minister, Angel Borlenghi) and the state employees' unions actively participated in the leadership of the CGT No. 2.[46]

The ideological balance of Argentina's union leaders had always tilted heavily to the left. The programmatic goals of the CGT and the USA placed special emphasis upon the need for fundamental structural change: the replacement of Argentina's capitalist system with state or cooperative ownership of the means of production and the concomitant development of a system of government under whose protection the working class could assert its right to participate in and eventually control the nation's destiny. Since 1936 the CGT had been affiliated with the Socialist Federación Sindical Internacional and the Confederación de Trabajadores de la América Latina (CTAL). Only the small Federación de Asociaciones Católicas de Empleadas (FACE) stood up for "God, Fatherland, Family, and Property."[47]

With these radical alternatives as an ideological backdrop for labor's more immediate financial concerns, Perón undoubtedly played upon the growing fears of Argentina's bourgeoisie when he spoke to an audience of concerned capitalists in 1944. "We wish . . . to eliminate from the labor organizations those extremists whose ideologies are so exotic to us . . . because of their foreign nature which we, the Argentines, have never felt inclined to support, and because they, with their sediment of ancestral hate, bring problems that neither interest nor concern us."[48] Perhaps one ancillary explanation of Perón's remarkable success was his ability to convince Argentina's middle class that he offered the only viable alternative to a socialist working-class revolution led by radical unions.

Prior to 1943 government indifference and union disorganization, combined with employer hostility, resulted in a politically weak working class. Between 50 and 70 percent of the industrial labor force was totally unorganized, and many of today's labor giants, including the metal and textile workers' unions, existed

principally on paper or simply did not exist at all.[49] In 1939, a representative year for which fairly reliable statistics are available, only 436,609 Argentines maintained union membership. Of this number 270,320 were affiliated with the CGT, and five unions representing the railroad workers (105,000 members), the construction workers (40,000 members), the commercial workers (35,000 members), and the streetcar workers (15,000 members) accounted for 72 percent of all CGT membership. None of the other forty-six CGT affiliates had attracted more than 10,000 members. The USA was even weaker numerically, with only 26,980 members dispersed among no fewer than forty-five affiliate unions, none of which was larger than 3,200 members.[50] With these data as evidence, one astute observer of Argentina's union movement concluded that before Perón "the mass of workers were indifferent [to labor organizing.] Except in the Unión Ferroviaria, in La Fraternidad, in the construction workers union, and in another that we cannot remember, only a minimal percentage of the workers joined a union.
. . . The leaders passed the time analyzing which was better: communism, democracy, or socialism."[51]

The turning point in the development of Argentine organized labor came in 1943, when the colonel's revolution of June offered one of its principal instigators the flexible circumstances propitious for political change. Following the trajectory of the labor movement since then, one sees that a decision was made to wrest political control from existing power holders by increasing working-class participation. The agency charged with implementing this decision was the Secretaría de Trabajo y Previsión, created in November 1943 out of the dormant Departamento Nacional de Trabajo and similar provincial bureaucracies which until then had been semi-autonomous dependencies of the Interior Ministry.

It is hardly possible, as Fayt has asserted, that Perón merely acted as a figurehead, signing decrees and mouthing the speeches of his lieutenants.[52] The Secretariat was the job Perón deliberately chose for himself, and he obviously controlled its increased activity and power. Staffed by such dependable associates as Lt. Col. Domingo Mercante (Director de Trabajo y Acción Social Directa) and Juan Atilio Bramuglia (Director de Previsión Social), the Secretariat soon expropriated the Buenos Aires city council building for its headquarters, prompting the resignation of the newly appointed mayor.[53] After 17 October 1945, Mercante assumed control of the Secretariat, and it became the "basic driving force of the campaign that would carry [Perón] to the Presidency. . . . It was a super-committee that compensated for the lack of newspapers, the improvised political organization, and the shortage of money that harassed Perón's campaign."⁵⁴ Even the short-lived Peronist Partido Laborista was founded and organized by the Secretariat.

A serious obstacle to the development of the labor movement as a powerful force was the disorder within the CGT. The government quickly decreed the dissolution of the CGT No. 2, and soon thereafter dealt the CGT No. 1 a severe blow by intervening its powerful affiliates, the railroad workers' unions. The two navy captains named as interventors forced the rail unions and José Domenech to withdraw from the CGT No. 1. In October, Perón replaced both interventors with Colonel Domingo Mercante, the son of a retired locomotive engineer. Then, with the nation's central labor federations virtually dissolved, Perón proceeded to rebuild the CGT as his personal power base, paying special attention to the recruitment of capable leaders. A truly gifted persuader, Perón had little difficulty convincing many unionists of his sincerity in wishing to construct a powerful independent union movement. Established leaders, such as Luis Gay, Angel Borlenghi, and David Diskin, joined such relative newcomers as Cipriano Reyes and Luis Monzalvo, in active support of the man who promised not only material benefits but also the opportunity to participate in deciding what those benefits might be. In addition, an entire corps of new leaders needed to be created in the nonunionized industries and in replacement of the leaders, mostly socialists, who refused to cooperate with the insistent colonel.

Using the carrot, the stick, and a large dose of imagination, Perón pursued union reorganization with uncommon zeal. The intervened Unión Ferroviaria provided him with an initial success when a group of obscure men from subordinate leadership levels led by Luis Monzalvo successfully claimed majority support among the union's rank and file. Since the government's intervention of August 1943, the union had had no leaders. Apparently, Perón ordered Mercante to canvass all eligible candidates and produce the ones most likely to prove both competent and malleable. These new leaders were then given wide publicity and slowly eased into the union's leadership. No nominations were made; no elections were held.

Uncooperative unions had increasingly fewer possibilities of successfully defying Perón. José Peter's communist Federation of Workers of the Meat Industry had no intention of cooperating with the military government after struggling alone and unsuccessfully for more than a decade to organize the employees of Argentina's packing plants. In the midst of a rain of favorable wage settlements forced by the Secretariat, the meat workers found that Peter's energetic bodyguard, Cipriano Reyes, had formed a rival Federation of Labor Unions of the Meat Industry. Carefully nurtured by Perón and Mercante, Reyes's federation soon eliminated its competitor and in the process finally organized the vast majority of packing house workers.

In addition to renovating the leadership of established unions and encouraging the development of parallel unions to outmaneuver recalcitrant ones, Perón also provided the initial organizational impetus for dozens of unions of undeniable importance in contemporary Argentina. Membership in the metalworkers' union mushroomed astoundingly under Perón's tutelage, reaching more than 100,000 by 1947. From this base it would become the backbone of the Argentine labor movement in the post-1955 era. Other successful organizational efforts included the Tucumán Federation of Sugar Industry Workers, founded in mid-1944, with 100,000 members by 1947; the Union of Wood Industry Workers (founded late 1944; 35,000 members by 1947); the Union of Construction Workers (September 1943; 30,000 members by 1947); and the Union of Bakery Personnel (November 1943; 20,000 members by 1947). Not even the jockeys at Palermo's racetrack were beyond the Secretariat's enthusiastic organizers.

The outlines of Perón's labor policies had become obvious long before September 1945, but it was only then that his political rivals began to react strongly. The Socialists used what little remaining influence they had in the labor movement to urge individual unions to withdraw from the Peronist CGT. On September 6 La Fraternidad left the CGT, and was soon followed by the textile workers' and the shoe workers' unions as well as by important factions of the General Confederation of Commercial Employees and the trolley car workers' union. With the exception of La Fraternidad, Perón moved quickly to construct rival unions, and the rebel organizations soon found themselves isolated. The breakaway Unión Obrera Textil was replaced in the CGT by a more docile Asociación Obrera Textil, and whereas the former had united 2,000 workers in 1943, the latter boasted of 85,000 members in 1946. In January 1946, the Socialist Sindicato de la Industria del Calzado discovered a competitor in the new Peronist Unión Obrera de la Industria del Calzado, which rapidly grew to more than 18,000 members.

In October 1945, to further insure that the Socialist reaction never reached dangerous proportions, Perón—now vice-president, minister of war, president of the National Postwar Council, as well as secretary of labor and welfare—issued Decree 23,854, the Law of Professional Associations. According to the decree's provisions, not only could there be but one union per industry but the selected union needed official recognition from the Secretariat of Labor and Welfare. Without a government-granted *personería gremial*, a union was effectively prohibited from functioning. Unions without recognition, for example, could not hold a meeting in private or public without police approval, which in practice was rarely obtainable. Once *personerías* had been granted to their new Peronist rivals, the rebel shoe and textile unions simply could not continue to exist. Similar use of the Law of Professional Associations later ruined the hotel and restaurant workers', the shipbuilders', the printers', the clothing workers', and the maritime workers' unions, among others, and demonstrated Perón's intolerance of deviation from his directives.

Perón was always careful, however, to differentiate between the "corrupted" coteries of uncooperative union officials and the uncorrupted union membership. Because the high-handed treatment of union leaders was almost invariably accompanied by a *conquista social* for the union rank and file, and because Perón was uncommonly adept at fostering the appearance that he had rescued the misled workers from betrayal, his popularity among members of the working class apparently suffered very little.

In other words, a basic distinction should be made between the Argentine union movement and the Argentine union member when assessing the nature of Peronism. Perón was no friend of an independent labor movement, but he was a great friend of the working class, the best it has ever had, and apparently the loss of union autonomy was not too dear a price for such a remarkable friendship. Cipriano Reyes once suggested that Perón had lost much of his unionized following by 1955 and that he never would have been victorious in the free elections scheduled for 1957.[55] But, as José Luis de Imaz has stated, "while it is true that Perón and his political machine occasionally decided who the leaders of certain unions should be, and that no one could be a leader without Perón's approval, regardless of the process actually followed, the interests of unionized labor were heard, and the size of the unions grew significantly. Whether the procedure to select labor spokesmen was democratic or not (and very often it was not), the net results were pleasing to the majority of the rank and file."[56]

Certainly a substantial portion of working-class political participation during the Perón government was symbolic—what Worsley
would call "pseudo-intervention"—but it is impossible to reduce
the matter to a simple question of whether the workers sold their
right to participate independently in politics for a basket of material
and psychic benefits.[57] Regardless of one's interpretation of Perón,
working-class participation under Peronism was far, far higher
than under rival liberal governments. Before Perón, during the
anti-Peronist interregnum (1955–73), and since 1976, liberal governments have consistently mocked working-class political participation by proscribing candidates, annulling elections, and overthrowing legitimate governments. Small wonder, then, that many
workers recall the Perón administrations as their golden age of
political participation.

The length of this discussion of the Argentine working class
should not be permitted to obscure the fact that while the backbone
of the Peronist coalition has always been the urban working class,
that support alone could never account for the Peronists' remarkable electoral strength—more than 60 percent of the popular vote
in the national election in September 1973. As noted above, between one-eighth and one-sixth of the Argentine middle class is
favorably oriented toward Peronism.

It is in the analysis of middle-class support for Peronism that the
policy disagreements between liberals and populists are placed in
the starkest relief. Certain sectors of the urban middle class were
created by or matured during the Peronist administrations, and
these sectors naturally tend to produce a disproportionate number
of loyal Peronists. Certainly the nonentrepreneurial white-collar
labor force, composed in large measure of government officials and
employees of state-financed or state-protected enterprises, views
Peronism with favor, for many of those jobs were also created
during Peronist administrations. So too does that part of the entrepreneurial middle class that profited from such Peronist economic
policies as tariff protection, a labor movement oriented toward
conciliation, and a host of expansion-inducing monetary and fiscal
policies, particularly liberal access to government credit at below-
market interest rates. Finally, support for Peronism comes from
those Argentines—not restricted to the urban middle class—who
view growth and development as paramount national objectives.
A former assistant secretary of state for inter-American affairs
noted in 1981 that the achievement of these objectives, variously
called modernization, development, economic rationality, and

even national security, "is what political dynamics are about in Latin America today."[58] It is what political dynamics have been about for the past four decades in Argentina.

It is important to note that the Peronist coalition of the 1970s was singularly broad, for it included two new groups: military leaders and businesspeople with a stake in stability, on the one hand, and leftist guerrillas, on the other. The latter group became active in 1969, and soon thereafter had succeeded in traumatizing the majority of Argentines who value political stability. The *cordobazo* and, perhaps more important, the murder of expresident Pedro Aramburu are widely believed to have signaled a major shift in the thinking of many military officers.[59] Rising guerrilla activity and labor militancy (characterized by that of Augustín Tosco's light and power workers in Córdoba and Raimundo Ongaro's CGT de los Argentinos) led to a move toward conciliatory Peronism and away from the discredited confrontational policies of the Onganía period. Peace was made with Perón by the promise of free elections, and as the Peronist electoral machinery cranked up, support for the more radical, nonconciliatory labor factions quickly faded.

At about the same time, the guerrilla left changed its tactics as well. It ceased the struggle to replace Peronism and began to focus upon taking over the Peronist movement. Infiltration meant inclusion in the national populist coalition of groups that shared some of the long-standing Peronist values but that fundamentally rejected the Peronist orientation toward class conciliation. True to his past, however, Perón accepted any support for the upcoming electoral battle, and in fact it was these radical-left groups that served as the mobilizing force behind the 1973 Peronist electoral victories. The Juventud Peronista (JP) was formed in 1972, largely out of the university-oriented Juventud Argentina por la Emancipación Nacional (JAEN), and the JAEN's leadership (particularly Rodolfo Galimberti) effectively shared with Perón the control of the JP. The outright guerrilla groups—the Montoneros, the Fuerzas Armadas Peronistas, and the Fuerzas Armadas Revolucionarias—also came under the Peronist umbrella.[60]

No coalition encompassing both groups oriented toward stability and the radical guerrilla left can long endure, of course, and the national populist coalition of the 1970s began to disintegrate almost before it was formed. The massacre at Ezeiza Airport in June 1973 is generally thought to have been a sharp warning to the left by the conciliatory labor sector, and from that date on, the left was slowly excluded from the coalition. In January 1974 Perón himself attacked the JP at a meeting of right-wing youth groups, and the following May he launched a verbal assault on the JP and the Montoneros during his traditional May Day speech in the Plaza de Mayo. Two months after Perón's death, the Montoneros announced that they were resuming guerrilla activities.[61]

Once the left had been ejected, the coalition began to disintegrate further, and it did so for much the same reason that its predecessor had failed two decades earlier: in an era of low growth the government could not respond satisfactorily to the diverse demands of a heterogeneous coalition, and intensifying class conflict over severely limited resources rendered the government impotent. Early in his last administration, Perón negotiated a Social Contract in which labor and management agreed to cooperate in moderating their demands for wage and price increases. As Gary Wynia has noted, the Peronist Social Contract can be divided into two periods. The first ended shortly before Perón's death in mid-1974 and coincided with an economic boomlet. The second coincided with a rising oil import bill ($58 million in 1972; $588 million in 1974) which "contributed to raw-product shortages, the slowing of economic growth, and the disaffection of raw-product-consuming industrialists."[62] Facing this decay, the Isabel Perón government moved steadily to the right, in the process deserting its working-class base. It thereby destroyed the legitimacy of its claim to public office. Facing a defenseless adversary, the liberals once again easily overthrew a populist constititional government.

CHAPTER 3

PERONIST ELECTORAL SUPPORT:

A MULTIVARIATE ANALYSIS

Social class is clearly the premier variable in explaining the nature of Peronist electoral support. But it is unwise to place exclusive emphasis upon this single factor, for a significant proportion of the working class has never supported Peronism. And as the preceding chapter demonstrated, a healthy proportion of the middle class has also supported Peronism. What makes these class-based correlations less than perfect? What features other than social class are associated with support for the Peronist movement? And, more important, what is the relative influence of these features upon one another, upon social class, and upon support for Peronism?

This chapter attempts to answer these questions first by examining the independent influence of three important clusters of variables: demographic change, industrial development and growth, and economic satisfaction. Then a multivariate analysis links these clusters to variations in social class and in support for the Peronist movement. The fundamental goal of this analysis is to construct a simple model that accurately describes the effect of socioeconomic variables upon the populist vote. Unfortunately, the path to this simple model is somewhat complex, and I must ask for the reader's patience. While some of the tables in this chapter may be difficult to decipher, the discussion in the text requires nothing more than a willingness to read slowly.

DEMOGRAPHIC CHANGE

Demographic variables have often been used to explain variations in patterns of political behavior, but the traditional view that posited a direct, often linear progression from demographic shifts (particularly urbanization) to economic frustration, social disorientation, and, eventually, radical political activity is now quite dead, the victim of its own oversimplification. Of course demographic change has not been abandoned as a variable capable of explaining alterations in political behavior, but most contemporary studies place greater emphasis upon the interdependence of apparently discrete phenomena that *together* affect politics. Karl Deutsch's seminal study utilizes four demographic variables (change in locality of residence, population growth, occupational shift out of agriculture, and change from rural to urban residence) to operationalize his concept of social mobilization. But in using these variables he emphasizes that "the first and main thing about social mobilization is . . . that it does assume a single underlying process of which particular indicators represent only particular aspects."[1]

Most research on the political correlates of demographic change now challenges the existence of direct linkages to political behavior. In his six-nation comparative study of the impact of the factory upon participant attitudes of workers, for example, Alex Inkeles found urbanization to be of limited explanatory value: "When matching controlled for the amount of factory work a man had, not much predictive power remained in the measure of years of urban experience."[2] Norman H. Nie, G. Bingham Powell, Jr., and Kenneth Prewitt employed data from Gabriel Almond and Sidney Verba's *Civic Culture* study to observe that it is not urbanization but social stratification and organizational membership that affect political participation.[3] Wayne Cornelius has persistently questioned the wisdom of a descriptive literature that utilizes migration and urbanization as variables to account for Latin American political instability.[4] The general consensus is that demographic change is only one of several processes that act in concert to effect changes in political behavior.

One of these processes seems particularly relevant to Argentina's populist experience: the integrative efforts of secondary associations, specifically labor organizations. The wave of migrants that flooded Buenos Aires during the Depression and World War II was received with enmity by the existing industrial labor force, whose members resented the pressures new job applicants placed upon wage levels.[5] In the conventional view these migrant masses languished in an institutional vacuum until they were resurrected as Perón's *descamisados*. The voluminous literature on Peronism is packed with references to unassimilated migrants whose crude mental processes and feeble social position made them susceptible to paternalistic leaders bearing gifts of material and psychic gratification.[6]

Conjectures of this type form the foundation of nearly every analysis of the Peronist movement. For example, Carlos Fayt states that Perón's success depended upon "the indifference and the availability of the new sectors of recent rural extraction without any union experience." According to Tomás Roberto Fillol, "the loss of traditional forms of security makes migrant workers eager to find new reference groups with which to identify. . . . The result is the formation of a rootless human mass eager to follow any leader capable of supplying them with a new and attractive set of values and ideals. For such people, Perón's demagoguery had an almost compulsive appeal."[7]

Little evidence has been offered to corroborate such statements, however. In fact Perón himself seemed to contradict them when he asserted that the largest and most powerful union in Argentina, the Unión Ferroviaria, "represented the initial nucleus of our revolutionary movement."[8] Such unsubstantiated generalizations as those above should be measured against the results of research throughout Latin America which demonstrate that the transition from rural to urban environments is not particularly disruptive of traditional norms, values, and behavior patterns.[9]

Demographic change has always shared with social class the leading position on any list of variables crucial to an adequate explanation of the development of the Peronist phenomenon. Here again, however, descriptive analyses have tended either to blend discrete demographic characteristics—migrants "uprooted from their native environment and out of place in the new"[10]—or, more frequently, to place demographic variables alongside other socioeconomic variables without attempting to assess their separate effects: "These displaced persons were not only poor and resentful; coming from the interior, where the Indian strain had been strong in colonial and early national times, they were also so swarthy that most of the older *porteños* referred to them contemptuously."[11]

Early in the data preparation a factor analysis of the demographic variables indicated the existence of two distinct demographic dimensions. The first, urbanization, maintained a correlation of $+.10$ with the second, somewhat broader category, population growth (POPULATION GROWTH), which was defined as the percent average annual population increase and the percent average annual change in population density.[12] Although migrants undoubtedly contributed to the area's population growth, no reliable data have ever been found to document their proportional share of the overall population increase.[13] Urbanization was simply defined as the percent of a county's or ward's total population living in population clusters of two thousand or more persons in the census years of 1947 and 1960.

Given that by 1960 Greater Buenos Aires, with its eight million inhabitants, was vying with Mexico City for the distinction of being the largest Spanish-speaking metropolis on earth, the area's negligible variation in percent urban population renders meaningless an analysis of the independent influence of urbanization upon the Peronist vote. While it is true that in 1947 and even in 1960 there was considerable variation in the percent urban population among Greater Buenos Aires's counties—the mean percent urban in 1947 was 92 percent with a range from 42 to 100 percent—social scientists nevertheless define urbanization broadly as the *exposure* to an urban environment through media, economic interaction, or physical proximity. By this definition the entire population of Greater Buenos Aires has long been as urban as any in the world. Given its insufficient variance, then, urbanization was eliminated from this study.

The literature on populism indicates that the second dimension of demographic change, population growth, should maintain an important positive relationship with the Peronist vote. With a zero-order POPULATION GROWTH–PERON correlation of $+.69$, the data in Table 3.1 tend to confirm the findings of earlier studies. Because much of Buenos Aires's demographic change may be attributed to working-class migration from the interior, it is possible that a more fundamental association between social class and Peronism underlies the POPULATION GROWTH–PERON relationship. Apparently, population growth is more than just an intervening variable, however, for despite the $+.35$ WORKING CLASS–POPULATION GROWTH correlation, the first-order partial between POPULATION GROWTH and PERON controlling for WORKING CLASS remains a very high $+.70$. Only when controlling for the composite variable of INDUSTRIAL GROWTH (see Appendix) is the POPULATION GROWTH–PERON correlation reduced from $+.79$ to $+.08$. And here, unfortunately, the intractable problem of multicollinearity (the POPULATION GROWTH–INDUSTRIAL GROWTH correlation is $+.84$) distorts the meaning of partial correlation coefficients.

TABLE 3.1

Pearson Correlations between Population Growth and the Peronist Vote,
Greater Buenos Aires, 1946–1973 (N=39)

	PERON	1946	1954	1957	1960	1962	1965	1973
POPULATION GROWTH	.69	.65	.76	.67	.76	.73	.66	.64
% Average annual population growth								
1914–47	.76	.63	.71	.62	.66	.67	.62	.56
1947–60	.70	.44	.71	.64	.72	.72	.71	.78
% Average annual change in population density								
1914–47	.67	.63	.71	.63	.67	.67	.62	.56
1947–60	.70	.67	.70	.69	.68	.70	.63	.63

Source: Ministerio del Interior, Dirección Nacional Electoral; Dirección Nacional de Estadística y Censos, *Censo nacional de población 1960.*

INDUSTRIAL DEVELOPMENT AND GROWTH

The literature on the origin and persistence of Peronism hypothe-
sizes a direct linkage with an area's absolute level of industrialization, narrowly defined here in terms of factories and operational-
ized as the composite variable INDUSTRY.[14] Table 3.2 presents the
zero-order Pearson correlations between INDUSTRY, its component
variables, and the vote for the Peronist movement in Greater Buenos Aires.[15] As measured by the number of workers per industrial
establishment, wages per industrial establishment, and value of
production per industrial establishment, INDUSTRY seems to be
nearly unrelated to Peronist voting patterns. In 1946, and to a
lesser extent in 1957, a positive association exists between areas
containing large factories (workers per industrial establishment)
and those possessing substantial Peronist electoral strength, but
over time this relationship becomes insignificant.

The lack of substantial evidence to confirm the expected positive
relationship between an area's Peronist vote and its level of industrial development encourages a reinterpretation of the original hypothesis. A closer inspection of the literature reveals, in fact, that
the simple INDUSTRY–PERON linkage is offered as a harbinger of
changes not in an area's economic structure but rather in the nature of its social-class composition. No one suggests that industry
directly causes a large vote for Peronism; rather, industrial development tends to attract the types of persons, generally working-
class persons, who then go to the polls in support of the Peronists. If an area's working-class population is an intervening linking
variable between industrial development and the Peronist vote, a
partial correlation between INDUSTRY and PERON controlling for
WORKING CLASS will indicate the proportion of the +.15 zero-order
relationship that may be directly attributed to industrialization.
Not surprisingly, the first-order partial is −.37, demonstrating not
only that all of the positive influence of INDUSTRY on PERON is due
to the fact that industrialization attracts working-class voters but
also that industrialization actually has a negative effect upon the
Peronist vote. Should an area manage to industrialize without at-
tracting a disproportionately larger working-class population, it
will exhibit relatively anti-Peronist voting patterns. Because this
occurs so infrequently (the INDUSTRY–WORKING CLASS correlation is
+.45) the question need not be pursued beyond noting once more
the crucial influence of an area's working-class population upon its
electoral behavior.[16]

TABLE 3.2

Pearson Correlations between the Level of Industrialization and the Peronist Vote,
Greater Buenos Aires, 1946–1973 (N=39)

	PERON	1946	1954	1957	1960	1962	1965	1973
INDUSTRY	.15	.24	.07	.25	.06	.10	.15	.12
Workers per industrial establishment								
1935	.06	.23	−.06	.16	−.01	.03	.02	.02
1941	.15	.34	.11	.22	.03	.10	.13	.04
1947	.23	.38	.15	.32	.17	.18	.18	.15
1963	−.08	−.01	−.12	−.04	−.09	−.13	−.10	−.05
Wages per industrial establishment								
1935	−.13	−.03	−.26	−.04	−.17	−.14	−.12	−.13
1941	−.13	.01	−.19	−.05	−.22	−.16	−.11	−.17
1947	.04	.13	−.05	.12	.01	.01	.02	.01
1963	.00	.04	−.02	.02	−.02	−.03	.00	.02
Value of production per industrial establishment								
1947	.13	.26	.04	.22	.08	.11	.11	.07
1963	.20	.27	.18	.19	.17	.18	.17	.21

Source: Ministerio del Interior, Dirección Nacional Electoral; Comisión Nacional del Censo Industrial, *Censo industrial de 1935*; Dirección General de Estadística y Censos, *Estadística industrial de 1941*; Ministerio de Asuntos Técnicos, *IV censo general de la Nación*; Instituto Nacional de Estadística y Censos, *Censo nacional económico 1963*.

Outside Greater Buenos Aires are nearly five hundred counties possessing incredibly varied levels of industrialization: such major industrial centers as Rosario and Córdoba may be compared with counties inhabited by more glaciers than blue-collar workers. The zero-order correlations between the level of industrialization and the Peronist vote in these counties are presented in Table 3.3. Here again, INDUSTRY appears associated with neither positive nor negative Peronist electoral performance. No coefficient accounts for as much as 9 percent of the variation in the vote for Peronism.

Many observers have asserted that the economic basis of Peronism's electoral strength lies not in an area's level of industrial development or its type of industrial activity but rather in Argentina's differential levels of economic change. This process of economic change is said to initiate a complex series of interconnected socioeconomic and sociodemographic transformations which, taken together, encourage the development of populism. As narrowly defined here in terms of industrial growth, economic change acts as a catalyst to "detraditionalize" a region's social and political behavior.[17]

This hypothesis is supported by the Peronist electoral data. The Pearson coefficients in Table 3.4 indicate an extremely strong positive relationship between the rate of industrial growth and Peronist voting strength. These correlation coefficients also disclose that the areas that grew most rapidly between 1935 and 1941 were those that *least* supported Peronism in subsequent elections. This is due to dramatic transformations in several established patterns of industrial growth in the years following this prewar period. Areas that had evidenced negative industrial growth rates between 1935 and 1941 blossomed forth with an impressive expansion of industrial facilities. The Pearson correlation between increases in industrial establishments from 1935 to 1941 and increases from 1941 to 1947 is $-.70$. From 1935 to 1941 the annual average economic growth rate of Lanús ranked thirty-fifth among Greater Buenos Aires's thirty-nine counties, while from 1941 to 1947 it was sixth. Similar leaps occurred in General San Martín (twenty-ninth to third), Lomas de Zamora (thirty-third to seventh), and Tres de Febrero (thirteenth to second). Not all of this growth was concentrated in areas that subsequently provided strong Peronist electoral support, of course, but the correlations in Table 3.4 intimate that after 1941 increases in the numbers of industrial establishments and industrial workers became—and remain—the most reliable economic indicators of Peronist strength.

TABLE 3.3

Pearson Correlations between the Level of Industrialization and the Peronist Vote,
All Argentine Counties, 1946–1965

	1946	1954	1957	1960	1962	1965
Workers per industrial establishment						
1947	.14	.20	.15	.11	.20	.28
1963	.12	.09	.23	.25	.25	.13
Wages per industrial establishment						
1947	.13	.17	.22	.13	.25	.28
1963	.10	.07	.26	.29	.24	.17
Value of production per industrial establishment						
1947	.13	.10	.22	.13	.25	.09
1963	.06	.04	.21	.26	.27	.13
	(N=290)	(N=328)	(N=348)	(N=308)	(N=304)	(N=289)

Source: Ministerio de Asuntos Técnicos, *IV censo general de la Nación*; Dirección Nacional de Estadística y Censos, *Censo nacional de población 1960*.

Note: Excluding Greater Buenos Aires.

TABLE 3.4

Pearson Correlations between Industrial Growth and the Peronist Vote,
Greater Buenos Aires, 1946–1973 (N=39)

	PERON	1946	1954	1957	1960	1962	1965	1973
INDUSTRIAL GROWTH	.79	.66	.81	.74	.81	.77	.75	.74
% Average annual change in industrial establishments								
1941–47	.59	.58	.60	.58	.60	.60	.57	.44
1947–63	.80	.69	.78	.73	.82	.82	.75	.79
% Average annual change in industrial workers								
1941–47	.68	.58	.66	.68	.71	.69	.66	.58
1947–63	.64	.45	.64	.52	.68	.66	.61	.71
Variables *not* used in construction of the composite variable INDUSTRIAL GROWTH								
% Average annual change in industrial establishments								
1935–41	−.50	−.50	−.44	−.57	−.45	−.51	−.51	−.37
% Average annual change in industrial workers								
1935–41	−.45	−.31	−.34	−.52	−.45	−.47	−.48	−.44

Source: See Table 3.3.

But while it is difficult to deny that areas undergoing industrial growth tend to be areas of strong Peronist electoral support, it is also important to emphasize that the simple correlation coefficients in Table 3.4 do not indicate the amount of direct independent influence of an area's industrial change upon its Peronist vote. As the high coefficients in the independent variable correlation matrix indicate (see Appendix), an area undergoing industrial change also tends to have a relatively rapidly growing population, to be relatively working class in social composition, and to exhibit relatively little economic satisfaction. The question of the direct and indirect effects of industrial change upon populist electoral strength remains to be addressed below.

A similar analysis of the influence of indicators of industrial growth upon the Peronist vote in the counties outside Greater Buenos Aires did not match the strong correlations between industrial growth and the Peronist vote in the metropolitan area. Outside Greater Buenos Aires not a single zero-order correlation coefficient could account for as much as 10 percent of the vote for Peronism. Even when correlations were computed between PERON and the indicators of industrial growth for the ninety counties exhibiting more than the mean rate of industrial change, the results revealed nothing significantly different from zero. Only when the nine counties with more than five hundred industrial establishments were grouped apart did impressive coefficients finally begin to appear, and if Guilford's formula to deflate artificially high estimates obtained from small samples is employed, even these lost their strength.[18]

ECONOMIC SATISFACTION

Nearly all theories that attempt to explain the development of populism emphasize the influential role of economic dissatisfaction in exacerbating the tensions of traditional politics and reducing the perceived legitimacy of traditional political actors to the point that new political groups can obtain access to the arenas of power. Thus an entire literature exists which relates the growth and persistence of the Peronist phenomenon to Argentina's economic woes.[19] Little effort has been made to separate the independent influence of economic satisfaction from membership in the lower classes, however, and many studies define somewhat narrowly the types of persons who might be unhappy with their economic conditions. That the weighty economic burdens of Third World societies fall most heavily upon those shoulders least able to support them cannot be doubted; that the working class is the only dissatisfied social sector and that economic discontent influences Peronist electoral behavior are hypotheses in need of empirical support.

Of all the variables under discussion in this study, economic satisfaction is perhaps the least compatible with ecological analysis. Unlike social status, economic change, or population growth, economic satisfaction is a subjective phenomenon that simply cannot be measured accurately. The best that can reasonably be expected from aggregate data is a comparative analysis of similar groups which, through the grouping process itself, tends to hold constant a number of potentially significant intervening variables. Because the data for this volume are from a relatively industrialized area— Greater Buenos Aires—and because Peronism apparently finds its most substantial support among industrial workers, attention is confined to industrial employees (*obreros* and *empleados*) and their economic satisfaction is defined in the simplest of terms—wages. While the crudity of this estimating procedure is evident, it is not unreasonable to expect that in a relatively urban environment with well-developed means of communications, differential wage rates would tend to create groups with different levels of economic satisfaction.

Given these constraints, then, are variations in areas' levels of economic satisfaction associated with variations in Peronist electoral strength? The data in Table 3.5 indicate that a fairly strong negative relationship exists between economic satisfaction and the vote for Peronism. The simple Pearson correlation between SATIS-FACTION and PERON of −.47 tends to confirm earlier analyses linking economically dissatisfied voters to the Peronist movement. But a closer inspection of partial correlations casts doubt upon this relationship and suggests that the SATISFACTION–PERON linkage may be spurious. At issue here is the influence of the size of an area's working-class population upon both variables. Experience with urban immigrant concentrations in the United States and elsewhere has demonstrated that recent arrivals are generally forced to accept relatively low-status employment. Because much of the working class of Greater Buenos Aires is composed of internal migrants who are generally more satisfied with their new economic positions than with their former existence, it is imperative to analyze the influence of an area's working class upon its level of economic satisfaction.[20]

TABLE 3.5

Pearson Correlations between Economic Satisfaction and the Peronist Vote, Greater Buenos Aires, 1946–1973 (N=39)

	PERON	1946	1954	1957	1960	1962	1965	1973
SATISFACTION	–.47	–.60	–.50	–.49	–.42	–.44	–.38	–.33
Wages per industrial employee								
1935	–.34	–.45	–.38	–.37	–.29	–.31	–.26	–.24
1941	–.60	–.66	–.62	–.62	–.59	–.58	–.52	–.47
1947	–.42	–.53	–.43	–.46	–.35	–.40	–.35	–.30

Source: See Table 3.3.

As it turns out, areas that might be classified as economically satisfied tend to be areas exhibiting relatively small working-class populations: the SATISFACTION–WORKING CLASS correlation is −.54. Conversely, the areas of greatest Peronist voting strength have relatively large working-class populations: the WORKING CLASS–PERON correlation is +.77. For this reason, at any given level of working-class population, the first-order partial correlation between SATISFACTION and PERON plummets from −.47 to a nearly directionless −.11. In short, accepting the logic of the preceding paragraphs leads to the conclusion that economic satisfaction maintains only a marginal relationship with the Peronist vote.

Because its use would involve very tenuous assumptions, another independent variable—percent annual *increase* in wages per industrial employee—was omitted from the composite variable of economic satisfaction. But Perón has often been described as a vote-buyer, and for that reason alone the data in Table 3.6 deserve mention. They indicate what many have long assumed to be true: a substantial change occurred in the relationship between Peronist voting strength and increases in wages per industrial employee as Peronism began to attract workers in areas noted for their wage increases. This does not mean that Peronism's constituency changed; rather it suggests that the economic position of the same constituency was altered dramatically in a brief period. The correlation between increases in wages from 1935 to 1941 and increases in wages from 1941 to 1947 is −.42, demonstrating that the beneficiaries of earlier wage increases lost their relatively advantageous position after 1941. Perhaps more illuminating than this summary measure is a glance at specific areas. From 1935 to 1941 industrial employees in Buenos Aires's relatively wealthy Socorro received an average annual hike in wages per capita of 3.4 percent compared to negative adjustments in wages per capita in working-class areas such as General San Martín (−1.5 percent), Lanús (−3.8 percent), and Lomas de Zamora (−7.0 percent) during the same period.[21] Between 1941 and 1947 these roles were reversed, as Socorro's substantial average annual wage increase of 8.2 percent was more than matched by the three working-class counties' average of 11.3 percent. For those employees accustomed to wage reductions, the increase might have appeared even greater.

TABLE 3.6

Pearson Correlations between Industrial Wage Increases and the Peronist Vote,
Greater Buenos Aires, 1946–1973 (N=39)

% Average annual increase in wages per industrial employee	PERON	1946	1954	1957	1960	1962	1965	1973
1935–41	-.51	-.38	-.47	-.52	-.58	-.52	-.54	-.50
1941–47	.54	.43	.54	.55	.61	.50	.47	.47
1947–63	.22	.21	.26	.21	.22	.25	.21	.26

Source: See Table 3.3.

MULTIVARIATE ANALYSIS

It should now be possible to assess the relative importance of these independent variables from a vantage point provided by our understanding of the manner in which they are individually associated with the vote for Peronism. The purpose here is not to construct and then to test a series of causal models in an attempt to explain Peronist electoral behavior. When the tendency of aggregate data to generate impressive correlation coefficients is combined with our not infrequent inclination to accept quantitative data at face value, it is possible that the results of an uncontrolled regresssion of PERON on all five composite independent variables (see Table 3.7) may be misinterpreted. Despite the impressive coefficient of determination, .86, this regression equation "explains" variance only in the statistical sense of the word. To employ these data as a substantive explanation of Peronism's voting behavior would be tacitly to presume not only that these aggregate data accurately reproduce individual-level attitudes and behavior but that the independent variables are all those most likely to determine the Peronist vote—presumptions many would consider untenable. Other variables which are not based entirely upon socioeconomic characteristics—party organization, factory experience, union membership, to name but a few—need to be included in any such explanatory model. While the purpose of this inquiry is somewhat less ambitious, it is an essential step toward eventual explanation: what is proposed is a clarification of only the socioeconomic basis of variation in Peronist voting patterns. It is assumed that socioeconomic variables contribute an unknown amount toward an understanding of the movement's electoral behavior. It is assumed that most, if not all, of the socioeconomic variables have been identified.[22] We wish to determine which among them are the most influential.

This tentative understanding of the manner in which the variables relate to one another is in large measure derived from deductive theory and the preceding discussions of hypothesized associations rather than from the data themselves. The purpose of this multivariate approach, therefore, is not to employ causal inference to reduce a large number of logical models to one or more optimum explanatory sequences. Rather it is to propose a fixed model and then to determine the relative influence of each of the model's linkages. The procedures followed here do not begin with the development of prediction equations specifying zero relation-

TABLE 3.7

Uncontrolled Multiple Regression of PERON
on the Composite Independent Variables,
Greater Buenos Aires

Variable	R	R²	b/Beta[a]	Standard error b
INDUSTRIAL GROWTH	.79	.62	.49	.14
WORKING CLASS	.92	.84	.60	.11
SATISFACTION	.93	.86	.17	.09
POPULATION GROWTH	.93	.86	.14	.13
INDUSTRY	.93	.86	−.02	.09

a. Since each of the variables is standardized, the path coefficients are identical to the regression coefficients.

ships, then, but take a given model and compute the path coefficients. With the causal order fixed, no linkages will be eliminated. This seems only logical in the present context, where the goal is to analyze variables representing specific hypotheses found throughout the literature on Peronism and to determine which among them are most important and which have relatively little effect on the Peronist vote.

The core hypothesis that informs the basic socioeconomic model is that the rate of industrial growth is the fundamental independent variable acting directly and indirectly to influence the proportion of an area's Peronist vote. Figure 3.1 presents this causal model, and the appropriate path coefficients are given in Table 3.8. The large number of paths in Figure 3.1 should not be allowed to obscure some of the most important linkages, particularly the influence of INDUSTRIAL GROWTH upon PERON, WORKING CLASS, and POPULATION GROWTH, as well as the impact of WORKING CLASS upon both PERON and SATISFACTION. Table 3.8 indicates that industrial growth and working-class population totally dominate this six-variable model of Peronist electoral behavior.

Given the nature of the data, it is extremely difficult to separate the influence of industrial growth and population growth upon Peronist voting patterns. Although these two variables undoubt-

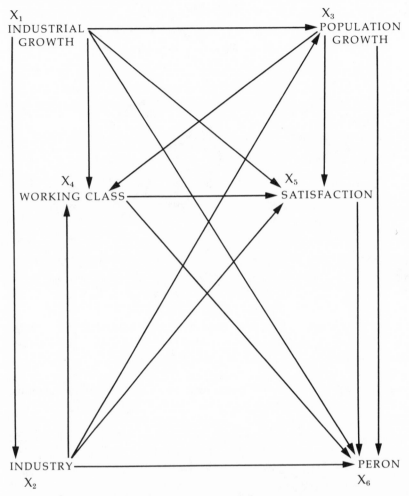

FIGURE 3.1. Six-Variable Causal Model: Paths from Industrial
Growth to the Peronist Vote

edly reinforce one another, one intuitively suspects that an area's
population would grow in response to industrial growth rather
than vice versa. In any event, it is upon this logic that we must rely,
for the POPULATION GROWTH–INDUSTRIAL GROWTH correlation of
+.84 renders the magnitudes of the regression coefficients nearly
impossible to assess.

One of the most intriguing questions raised by this model is the
extent to which the rate of industrial growth directly influences the

TABLE 3.8

Path Coefficients for Figure 3.1

Dependent Variable Equation	B_1	B_2	B_3	B_4	B_5
$X_6 = B_{61}X_1 + B_{62}X_2 + B_{63}X_3 + B_{64}X_4 + B_{65}X_5 + e_6$	.512	−.071[a]	.044[a]	.709	.201
$X_5 = B_{51}X_1 + B_{52}X_2 + B_{53}X_3 + B_{54}X_4 + e_5$	.029[a]	.288[a]	−.236[a]	−.607	
$X_4 = B_{41}X_1 + B_{42}X_2 + B_{43}X_3 + e_4$	.605	.564	−.066[a]		
$X_3 = B_{31}X_1 + B_{32}X_2 + e_3$	.830	−.031[a]			
$X_2 = B_{21}X_1 + e_2$	−.208				
$X_1 = e_1$					

Note: X_1 = INDUSTRIAL GROWTH; X_2 = INDUSTRY; X_3 = POPULATION GROWTH; X_4 = WORKING CLASS; X_5 = SATISFACTION; X_6 = PERON.
a. Path coefficients with associated regression coefficients less than twice their standard errors.

Peronist vote. In Table 3.9 an attempt has been made to determine the relative influence among the various paths from INDUSTRIAL GROWTH to PERON by first arriving at a basic correlation between industrial growth and PERON by summing the pathways of greatest theoretical interest. These pathways are the products of the path coefficients along each given path. With the basic correlation determined, the proportion of the correlations between INDUSTRIAL GROWTH and PERON attributable to various pathways can be calculated.[23] Nearly 52 percent of the correlation is accounted for by a direct linkage. Linkages passing through the demographic variable (POPULATION GROWTH) and the other economic variables (INDUSTRY and SATISFACTION) scarcely appear to affect the relationship between industrial growth and the Peronist vote. More than 43 percent of the basic INDUSTRIAL GROWTH–PERON correlation may be attributed to a path through WORKING CLASS, the single social structure variable.

Figure 3.2 is a simplified version of the same model which reflects the relative importance of the various independent variables. All path coefficients of less than .200 have been omitted; all those of more than .200 but less than .500 are indicated by broken lines; and all those of .500 and over are indicated by solid lines. The three independent variables that maintain direct links to PERON in Figure 3.2 (INDUSTRIAL GROWTH, WORKING CLASS, and SATISFACTION) account for all but 1 percent of the total variation in the Peronist vote that can be attributed to these socioeconomic variables. The addition of INDUSTRY and POPULATION GROWTH increases the coefficient of determination from .856 to .863.

It is difficult to overestimate the combined influence of an area's rate of industrial growth and the size of its working-class population upon Peronism's electoral behavior. By themselves they explain 84 percent of the total variation in PERON, or slightly more than 97 percent of the variation in PERON explained by all five independent variables.

CONCLUSION

These data provide a number of insights into the socioeconomic determinants of populist electoral behavior. Prime among these is the crucial role assumed by industrial growth in (1) directly contributing to an area's populist voting strength, and (2) inducing

TABLE 3.9

Proportional Components of the Relationship between Industrial Growth and the Peronist Vote, Greater Buenos Aires

Proportion of Basic Correlation Attributable to:		Path Coefficients	Percentage
Direct link to PERON		.512	52.0
Indirect link through demographic variable:			
INDUSTRIAL GROWTH → POPULATION GROWTH → PERON		.036	3.7
Indirect links through other economic variables:			
INDUSTRIAL GROWTH → INDUSTRY → PERON	.014		
INDUSTRIAL GROWTH → INDUSTRY → SATISFACTION → PERON	−.011		
INDUSTRIAL GROWTH → SATISFACTION → PERON	.005		
		.008	0.8
Indirect link through WORKING CLASS		.428	43.5
Basic correlation between INDUSTRIAL GROWTH and PERON		.984	100.0

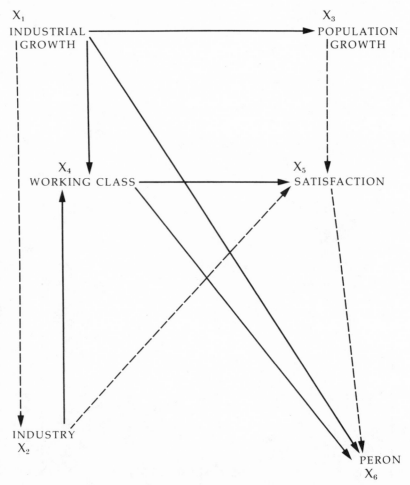

FIGURE 3.2. Six-Variable Causal Model: Selected Paths from
Industrial Growth to the Peronist Vote

changes in an area's social-class composition which, in turn, also
dramatically affect the vote for populist political movements.

One of the most persistent questions to arise out of the theoretical literature on social and political mobilization in the Third World
concerns the specific impact of economic variables upon political
behavior. At the center of this study is an inquiry into the direct
and indirect ability of one crucial variable—the rate of industrial
growth—to produce a particular type of political participation, that

is, electoral support for populist movements. In Argentina industrial growth not only exerts an impressive direct influence upon the level of the populist vote but substantially (beta = +.605) adds to an area's working-class population as well. Once this has occurred, these two independent variables then explain an extremely large percentage (84 percent) of the vote for Peronism.

The data also provide insight into the negligible influence of other variables often considered of primary importance in determining the populist vote. An area's level of industrial development, in particular, maintains no strong direct relationship with its populist electoral strength, although it does tend to exhibit a significant indirect influence through its ability to attract large numbers of working-class voters. This may seem so obvious as to merit scant mention, but factory experience per se is believed to be a crucial link in the creation of a participant working class. Factories are Inkeles's "schools for citizenship."[24] Thus the absence of a relationship between industrial development and populism suggests either that the factory does not develop participant citizens or, more likely, given the thoroughness of Inkeles's study, that the factory creates styles of participation which, relatively speaking, reject populism. While the data in this volume hardly bear comparison to those of Inkeles and Smith, they do provide the foundation for justifying future analyses of an entirely unexpected association.

These data also suggest an interesting insight into the relationship between a demographic variable, population growth, and populist electoral behavior. No doubt part of the negligible direct association between population growth and the vote for Peronism can be attributed to the inability of these data to distinguish between growth due to migration and nonmigratory increases in the resident population (see note 13). But population growth has long been thought to be closely linked to an area's vote for populist movements, for growth transmutes all too easily into instability, and, until recently, demographic instability in Third World environments carried with it the specter of anomic disposable masses willing to trade their votes and multiple anxieties for strong leadership from charismatic politicians. Now that we are aware of the pitfalls inherent in a macro-micro leap from growth to anomic political behavior (see note 20), there is no reason to expect to discover a direct association between population growth and the vote for populist political movements, and none was found in Argentina.

Finally, because these data appear to explain such a large proportion of the populist vote that may be attributed to socioeconomic variables, they provide the opportunity to suggest that future research into the phenomenon of populist mass support might now concentrate upon the amount of the total variation in the vote that can be explained by socioeconomic variables. This would involve the testing of models in which the variables presented here share prominence with other variables, particularly party organization and the differential impact of the often-mentioned *caudillo* ethic. Unlike many socioeconomic variables, most of these variables can be approached with reasonable confidence only through the use of survey data. Until the 1976 coup in Argentina, these data were increasing in quality, quantity, and availability.[25] Just as we have progressively refined our knowledge of the socioeconomic determinants of the populist vote since Germani's 1955 analysis of Peronist electoral behavior, so we might now begin to assess the relative worth of that knowledge in a broader universe of independent variables.

CHAPTER 4

PERONIST ELECTORAL CHANGE:

AN INDEX OF FLUIDITY

In the two preceding chapters several socioeconomic variables have been used to explain populist electoral behavior in Argentina. In those chapters the emphasis upon change was implicit: the analysis of correlation coefficients among elections over a period of twenty-seven years and the construction of indicators based upon time functions—the average annual increase in industrial establishments, for example. Explicit reference to the concept of change has been infrequent, however, because the relationship between Peronist electoral strength and the socioeconomic variables rarely seemed to vary significantly over the years.

In addition, the discussion of several types of change has been avoided because they cannot be explored with precision using aggregate data. One of these is electorate replacement, the simple result of aging, which creates enormous conceptual problems in any study spanning nearly three decades of political history. Aggregate data analysis cannot be used to determine precisely the number of Peronist voters in 1973 who were yet to be born in 1946, for example. With survey data, Butler and Stokes were able to separate changes that concern fundamental party alignments from those that involve responses to more immediate and transitory variables, such as candidate personality and issues of limited persistence.[1] But with aggregate data only the most circumspect separation of these two types of change is possible. Yet, they continue, a pessimistic outlook need not cloud aggregate analysis forever, since the explanations of individual behavior "often lie in a wider political or social milieu. Moreover, the consequences of individual change can be known only by aggregating the behavior of individual electors to see what is true of the electorate as a whole. Electoral analysis demands both the reduction or disaggregation of mass phenomena to individual terms and the aggregation of individual phenomena to explore effects in the full electorate."[2] The purpose of this chapter is to accept one part of this suggestion and explore electoral change within the aggregated Peronist electorate.

ELECTORAL VOLATILITY AND FLUIDITY

Aware of the hazards involved in making individual inferences from aggregate data, most Latin Americanists have chosen an extremely cautious approach to the analysis of electoral change in their region of specialization. In its most common form, this approach examines what may be termed electoral volatility—the net percentage gains and losses of individual parties between elections and, possibly, the trend over several elections. Unquestionably, such knowledge is highly important; but while useful as an accurate description of the *overall* pattern of a party's electoral performance, this measure of volatility can hide in its summary statistic a tremendously large number of possible combinations of percentage gains and losses from one election to the next. Take as an example the party that increases its share of the total vote from 20 percent to 25 percent between two elections. Here party support in the second election could indicate a voting switch by 5 percent to 45 percent of the electorate in the first election, as it is possible that any proportion of the proparty voters in the first contest switched to the opposition in the subsequent one. If aggregate data from only two elections are available, it is probably impossible to determine the type of changes that occur in any party's electoral performance.

If data are available from a relatively large number of elections, however, it is possible to *infer* a party's capabilities for defection and attraction over time through the construction of an index of fluidity based upon the analysis of districts' electoral volatility. This index is the sum of two probabilities, the probability of attraction (P_a) plus the probability of defection (P_d). The flow of voters *to* a party (here the various Peronist parties) may be expressed as the probability (P_a) that an antiparty voter in one election (X_{i-1}) will be attracted to the Peronist party in the subsequent election (X_i). Similarly, the flow of voters *away* from the Peronist party may be expressed as the probability (P_d) that a Peronist voter in election X_{i-1} will defect to the opposition in the subsequent election X_i. Since all data are in percentage units, the theoretical range of the index of Peronist electoral fluidity, $P_a + P_d$, is 0.0 to 2.0. The former figure represents complete stability, with neither attraction nor defection of voters between elections, while the latter represents complete fluidity, with 100 percent voter replacement between elections.

The next step is to determine the best estimate of the index for each of Argentina's electoral districts using data from the six elections between 1946 and 1965. One method to obtain such an estimate is to begin by expressing the vote for Perón in any election as a linear result of the vote in the previous election. Thus, the percentage Peronist vote in an election X_i would be equal to the percentage Peronist vote in the prior contest $[(X_{i-1})]$, *minus* all those voters who defected from the Peronist ranks between elections $[P_d(X_{i-1})]$, *plus* the voters who were attracted to the party from among all anti-Perón participants in the prior election $[P_a(1 - X_{i-1})]$, or

$$X_i = X_{i-1} - P_d(X_{i-1}) + P_a(1 - X_{i-1})$$

And then, by the simple algebraic process of gathering together all the X_{i-1} factors,

$$X_i = P_a + (1 - P_a - P_d) X_{i-1}$$

In this form, the vote for Perón in one election is a linear expression of the vote for Perón in the previous election, and the formula is identical to the familiar least squares regression equation, $y = a + bx$, in which the dependent variable y equals a constant (a, or the y intercept) plus the product of b (the regression coefficient) and the independent variable X. In particular,

$$b = 1 - P_a - P_d$$

and the index of electoral fluidity may therefore be expressed as

$$P_a + P_d = 1 - b$$

Using electoral data from all elections, at this point it becomes a simple matter to solve for b, subtract the result from 1, and obtain a best estimate of Peronist fluidity for each of the electoral districts in Argentina for which data are available (see Table 4.1). Here "best" is used in the least squares sense of the smallest sum of the squared deviations of the observed values from a best-fitting straight line. Or, for the future-oriented, with this technique the average squared error in prediction should be as small as possible given the constraints of the data.[3]

Before exploring the ways in which the index might be used to illuminate Peronist electoral behavior, it is appropriate to discuss some of the assumptions inherent in this mathematical model used to operationalize fluidity. One crucial assumption is that of constant probabilities—it is assumed that the *relative* size of an electoral district's switching pool ($P_a + P_d$) is unaffected by intervening variables peculiar to each election. Despite a considerable amount of electorate replacement through the process of aging, for example, the pool of voters contributing to electoral fluidity is presumed to remain constant or, more precisely, relatively constant

TABLE 4.1

Index of Fluidity

Area	Mean	Minimum	Maximum	Standard Deviation	N
Federal Capital	.721	.593	1.401	.080	208
Greater Buenos Aires	.752	.626	1.092	.240	39
All other counties	.858	.164	1.788	.099	314

when compared to all other electoral districts. Similarly, neither the proscription of the Peronist party nor the type of election, for the presidency, the legislature, or a constituent assembly, is taken into account by this model. The only way to avoid an assumption of constant probabilities is to weigh the data for each election in accordance with some scheme that orders the multitude of possible intervening variables in their ability to contaminate the model. Because so many intervening variables are involved, however, such a scheme will probably never be developed.

While the assumption of constant probabilities is obviously untenable, there are several characteristics of the Argentine political system that make the use of the index considerably less hazardous. First, voting is compulsory in Argentina and turnout regularly reaches about 90 percent of all eligible voters. This reduction in the number of sporadic voters is helpful, as casual voters generally contribute disproportionately to an electoral district's volatility. Eliminating this variable simply encourages the conceptualization of fluidity as a more constant pool of voters.

Of far greater importance, however, Argentine politics are personality dominated, and, significantly, the same personalities dominated them for the entire period encompassed in this study. Ignoring for a moment the obvious example of Perón himself, it is revealing that the two major presidential candidates in the first of two presidential elections in 1973 were the president of the Chamber of Deputies in 1948 and the UCR's presidential candidate in 1951. Nor is differential volatility encouraged by changing issues, for there is some research to indicate that only one issue divides the Argentine political parties, and that issue—what to do with the Peronists—is a significant one for the index of fluidity.[4] It suggests that since 1945 the only major cleavage in Argentine politics has been Peronism. In theory, a number of cross-cutting cleavages would encourage idiosyncratic vote switching, as party platforms attract and repel voters, but in fact the only (generally implicit) plank in any party platform that has differed from those of the platforms of all the other parties is that which concerns a policy toward Perón and the Peronists.

In short, because slow-changing, vague general principles strongly influence basic voter orientations and because the typical Argentine voter is apparently most comfortable when he or she can channel multiple political anxieties into what once seemed to be a perpetual personality struggle, the index's assumption of constant probabilities does less harm to reality in Argentina than it might elsewhere.[5] In spite of these rationalizations, however, it should be emphasized that the index of electoral fluidity is not perfect and will probably not provide precise transitional probabilities.

THE SOURCES OF PERONIST FLUIDITY

If fluidity is a function of the electorate's rational (in the Downsian sense of the word) response to perceived alterations in party performance, then certain factors that contribute to rational decision making should also contribute to relatively high levels of electoral fluidity. For example, the access to information provided by urbanization and modernization and the rational capabilities that relatively high levels of educational achievement imply should dictate high fluidity in areas demonstrating higher social-class composition as well as high levels of modernization and urbanization. On the other hand, if it is true that Argentine politics have been polarized for the past thirty-five years, then only those areas with high levels of economic or demographic instability should possess relatively high electoral fluidity, for the principal cause of fluidity would be the physical transformation of the electorate rather than a transformation of the electorate's attitudes.

Table 4.2 presents the zero-order correlations between the index of fluidity and three principal indicators of social class in each of the data sets. The very neutral coefficients from the Federal Capital are somewhat disappointing, for these are computed from the

TABLE 4.2

Pearson Correlations between Indicators of Social Class
and the Index of Fluidity

Indicator	Federal Capital	Greater Buenos Aires	All Other Argentine Counties
Occupation			
% Professionals, 1959	.00	−.43	
% Students, 1959	−.04	−.54	
% White-collar employees, 1959	.05	−.58	
% Businessmen, 1959	−.03		
% Blue-collar workers, 1959	−.11	.44	
% Unskilled laborers, 1959	.04		
Education			
% Illiterate adults, 1936		−.38	
% Illiterate age 14–21, 1943		.58	.34
% Illiterate parents, 1943		.43	.39
% Age 14–21 never completed grade school, 1943		.42	.41
% Age 6–13 not attending school, 1943		.21	.08
% Illiterate adults, 1947		.71	.39
% Urban illiterate, 1947			.36
% Illiterate adults, 1960	.09	.37	
Housing			
% Urban homes without public water, 1960		.73	.07
% Urban homes without toilets, 1960		.61	.35
% Urban homes without electricity, 1960		.70	.24

smallest units of analysis and the most reliable data. The conclusion is that occupation is not a useful explanatory variable for electoral fluidity in the Federal Capital. Outside the capital, it is evident that *areas demonstrating lower social-class composition also evidence high Peronist fluidity.* The coefficients from Greater Buenos Aires are generally much stronger than those from the other Argentine counties; yet even beyond the metropolitan boundaries the broad association seems discernible. With the exception of a single mysterious negative correlation for 1936 illiteracy levels, each of the twenty-three coefficients relates low social class to high fluidity or high social class to low fluidity, and several of the coefficients are among the strongest in this entire study.

In Table 4.3 a further set of correlations securely links *high* Peronist fluidity to five indicators of *low* levels of industrialization. While these data leave no doubt as to the direction of the relationship, it is worthwhile noting that in Greater Buenos Aires the association becomes weaker over time and in two cases (workers per industrial establishment and wages per industrial establishment) approaches neutrality. Since the index remains constant—there is only one index value for each electoral district—it must be that the relative level of industrialization has altered over time to the extent that *high fluidity is decreasingly related to low industrialization.* This hypothesis is congruent with earlier findings that indicated a disproportionate industrial and population growth in the relatively underpopulated and underindustrialized counties of Greater Buenos Aires. As the new, relatively dynamic industrial suburbs of Buenos Aires became increasingly capable of (statistically) balancing the influence of older areas within the capital and in counties such as Avellaneda, the association between low industrialization and high fluidity became less significant. Whether this fact can be attributed to the type of inhabitant of these growing industrial areas or whether it is simply a function of turnover of the electorate, in which the older residents (and the consistency of their electoral preferences) were submerged by new arrivals who voted differently, cannot be demonstrated by the present data. Logic suggests that the latter explanation might be quite reliable.

Although their significance appears somewhat weaker, the correlations in Table 4.4 indicate that the quality of industrialization is also negatively related to Peronist fluidity. Once again, the strong negative coefficients in 1935 for two indicators—electricity bought by industry and value of industrial production per industrial establishment—decrease over time to the point that the latter variable

TABLE 4.3

Pearson Correlations between Indicators of the
Level of Industrialization and the
Index of Fluidity

Indicator	Greater Buenos Aires	All Other Argentine Counties
Number of industrial establishments		
1935	−.55	−.34
1941	−.41	
1947	−.43	−.34
1963	−.24	−.32
Number of industrial workers		
1935	−.60	−.34
1941	−.56	
1947	−.57	−.25
1963	−.31	−.25
Workers per industrial establishment		
1935	−.45	−.17
1941	−.48	
1947	−.33	.15
1963	−.13	−.14
White-collar employees per industrial establishment		
1935	−.23	−.13
1941	−.37	
1947	−.19	−.03
1963	−.22	−.04
Wages per industrial establishment		
1935	−.37	−.13
1941	−.44	
1947	−.27	.08
1963	−.06	−.24

maintains a neutral relationship to electoral fluidity by 1963. The explanation for this phenomenon is quite probably the same as that offered in the preceding paragraph: electorate turnover is more powerful than changing attitudes in causing differential fluidity. This assumption appears congruent with the experience of Butler and Stokes in Britain, who found that although straight conversion played a dominant role in the period of British politics they studied, electorate replacement provided a continuous flow of new voters that consistently contributed disproportionately to electoral change.[6] These are conjectures, of course, but it is certainly evident that the established industrial areas throughout Argentina and especially in Greater Buenos Aires present very low levels of Peronist electoral fluidity. In addition, those newer industrial areas that were to become the Peronist movement's electoral backbone evidenced the nation's highest levels of fluidity, as new electorates took up residence in previously underindustrialized suburban counties.

This argument is supported by the data on demographic instability and urbanization in Table 4.5. In Greater Buenos Aires the wards and counties that have attracted the largest relative population growth and, especially, the largest relative number of internal migrants are the areas that evidence the highest levels of Peronist electoral fluidity. Considering the data in the preceding two tables, these data in Table 4.5 suggest that it is not industrialization per se but the demographic changes concomitant with industrialization that alter electoral patterns and thereby increase fluidity. This seems to be a satisfying explanation in view of the tremendous demographic shifts discussed in chapter 2.

The correlations in Table 4.6 relating Peronist electoral fluidity to levels of economic satisfaction provide very little insight into the role of this individual-level independent variable. One unexpected finding is that areas within Greater Buenos Aires that possess relatively large numbers of unemployed workers in 1947 also demonstrate low levels of fluidity. By 1947 there was virtually no unemployment in the capital and its suburbs, however: in none of the thirty-nine units was the unemployment rate higher than 2.4 percent, and the mean level rested at an enviable 1.6 percent with a standard deviation of 0.432. The extremely small variations in percent unemployed have obviously created a distorted picture of the relationship between fluidity and unemployment.

The other indicators of economic satisfaction display mixed associations with Peronist fluidity. In both Buenos Aires and the

TABLE 4.4

Pearson Correlations between Indicators of the
Quality of Industrialization
and the Index of Fluidity

Indicator	Greater Buenos Aires	All Other Argentine Counties
Electricity bought by industry		
1935	−.59	−.29
1947	−.46	−.18
1963	−.34	−.14
Value of production per industrial establishment		
1935	−.41	−.13
1947	−.35	−.11
1963	−.01	−.24
Horsepower per industrial establishment		
1935	−.18	−.14
1947	−.18	−.10
1963		−.20
Horsepower per industrial worker		
1935	−.05	.00
1947	−.01	−.16
1963	.19	−.01
Number of commercial establishments		
1947	−.44	−.24
1963	−.16	−.25

outlying counties high commercial wages indicate low electoral fluidity, while high industrial wages, on the other hand, are apparently unrelated to fluidity of any type. The percent annual increase in wages per industrial employee during the early Peronist era (1941–47) is positively but weakly related to high fluidity. Since wage increases were nearly uniform among all industrial workers

TABLE 4.5

Pearson Correlations between Indicators of
Demographic Instability and the Index of Fluidity

Indicator	Greater Buenos Aires	All Other Argentine Counties
% Average annual population growth		
1914–47	.25	
1947–60	.64	−.19
1960–70	.78	−.13
% Foreign born		
1947	−.36	−.34
1960	−.26	−.23
1970	−.51	−.27
Average annual change in % foreign born		
1947–60	.17	
1960–70	.26	
% Internal migrants		
1936	.52	
1947	.33	
% Born outside province of residence, 1947		
		−.28
% Average annual population growth through migration		
1914–47	−.22	−.18
1947–60	.74	−.29
Average annual change in % internal migrants, 1936–47	.31	

TABLE 4.6

Pearson Correlations between Indicators of
Economic Satisfaction and the Index of Fluidity

Indicator	Greater Buenos Aires	All Other Argentine Counties
% Economically active population unemployed, 1947	−.50	−.10
Wages per industrial employee		
1935	.10	−.03
1941	.01	
1947	.15	−.07
1963	.10	−.36
% Average annual increase in wages per employee		
1935–41	−.30	.09
1941–47	.32	
1947–63	.09	−.36
Wages per commercial employee		
1947	−.02	−.19
1963	−.42	−.35

during this period, the percent increases were weighted in favor of the lower-paid *obreros*, and so they were the most prominent contributors to the association between high fluidity and high wage increases. This same fact helps explain why in an earlier period (1935–41) when wage hikes were not uniform but rather frequently restricted to the Argentine labor elite, there is a negative correlation between fluidity and wage increases. Once more the relatively deprived are disproportionately large contributors to electoral fluidity.

Finally, Table 4.7 presents the relationship between Peronist fluidity and several indicators of industrial growth. In Greater Buenos Aires there are only two significant coefficients, and they not only are collinear but also refer to the same 1947–63 time period. If a judgment can be based upon these two indicators, it would appear that areas undergoing the most significant industrial growth dem-

TABLE 4.7

*Pearson Correlations between Indicators of Industrial Growth
and the Index of Fluidity*

Indicator	Greater Buenos Aires	All Other Argentine Counties
% Average annual change in industrial establishments		
1935–41	.09	.41
1941–47	.09	
1947–63	.44	−.31
% Average annual change in industrial workers		
1935–47	−.15	.24
1947–63	.62	−.40
% Average annual change in horsepower per worker		
1935–47	.18	−.03
1947–63	.12	.21
% Average annual change in commercial establishments		
1947–63		−.27

onstrate the highest levels of Peronist fluidity. This conclusion further encourages the belief that measures of industrial growth, and not absolute levels of industrialization and modernization, are those most capable of accounting for Peronist electoral fluidity. In Table 4.7 the data from outside Buenos Aires provide mixed coefficients, but the use of percentaged variables enables each indicator to be weighted strongly in favor of relatively rural counties. It is a fact, for example, that between 1935 and 1947 more than one *departamento* experienced a 100-percent increase in industrial establishments by adding two factories to the existing two.

Now that the relationship between fluidity and the seven principal independent variables have been discussed separately, perhaps the role of fluidity in Peronist electoral behavior would be clarified if another dependent variable, percent Perón, were introduced and the major findings from Table 4.2 through Table 4.7 ordered in their

TABLE 4.8

Greater Buenos Aires: Pearson Correlations of Selected Socioeconomic-Demographic
Indicators with Percent Perón, 1946–1965

Indicator	Percent Perón						
	1946	1954	1957	1960	1962	1965
Positive Correlation with Fluidity						
Low social class						
% Adult illiterate						
1947	.04	.41	.25	.38	.33	.32
1960	.75	.86	.80	.78	.86	.73
% Urban homes without public water						
1947	.51	.82	.65	.78	.78	.79
1960	.51	.78	.68	.73	.79	.70
Industrial growth						
% Ave. annual change in industrial workers,						
1947–63	.45	.63	.52	.68	.65	.64

Negative Correlation with Fluidity

High social class						
% Students, 1960	-.59	-.80	-.71	-.75	-.80	-.71
% Professionals and Executives, 1960	-.82	-.94	-.89	-.88	-.94	-.83
Quality of industrialization						
Electricity bought by industry, 1947	.46	.12	.35	.20	.23	-.09
Value of production per industrial establishment, 1935	.11	-.12	.12	-.05	-.01	-.14
Level of industrialization						
Number of industrial workers, 1935	.15	-.16	.07	-.12	-.09	-.31
Workers per industrial establishment						
1935	.23	-.06	.16	-.01	.02	-.05
1941	.33	.10	.22	-.05	.10	-.11

TABLE 4.9

*All Argentine Counties: Pearson Correlations of Selected Socioeconomic-Demographic
Indicators with Percent Perón, 1946–1965*

Indicator	Percent Perón						
	1946	1954	1957	1960	1962	1965	

Indicator	1946	1954	1957	1960	1962	1965
Positive Correlation with Fluidity						
Low social class						
% Age 14–21 never completed grade school, 1943	−.25	.42	−.29	−.27	−.15	.02
% Urban illiterate, 1947	−.24	.41	−.05	−.10	−.06	−.03
Economic change						
% Ave. annual change in industrial establishments, 1935–47	−.15	.20	−.12	−.06	.01	.12
Negative Correlation with Fluidity						
Industrial growth						
% Ave. annual change in industrial workers, 1947–64	.19	−.13	.12	.24	.12	−.12

Quality of industrialization						
Value of production per industrial establishment, 1964	.06	.04	.21	.26	.27	.13
Number of commercial establishments, 1947	.09	−.30	.21	.09	.05	.00
Level of industrialization						
Number of industrial workers, 1947	.14	−.18	.30	.13	.13	.02
Number of industrial establishments, 1963	.13	−.24	.23	.13	.06	−.05
Demographic instability						
% Foreign population, 1947	.38	.00	.09	.23	.22	.07
% Population born outside province of residence, 1947	.29	.00	.19	.23	.29	.14
Economic satisfaction						
Wages per commercial employee, 1964	.14	−.34	.16	.17	.13	−.06

influence upon fluidity. One way this might be accomplished is demonstrated by Tables 4.8 and 4.9. All indicators are included that contribute 1 percent or more to an increase in the squared multiple correlation coefficient (R^2): that is, any indicator which accounts for more than 1 percent of the total variation in fluidity among electoral districts when controlling for all the other indicators.

In many ways Table 4.8 is remarkable. It demonstrates with unprecedented clarity the strong connection between high fluidity and high electoral support for Perón in Greater Buenos Aires. In addition, those indicators associated with low fluidity are weakly or more frequently negatively related to Peronist electoral strength. Fluidity may be attributed either to electorate replacement or to changes in the electorate's vote, and, in fact, a substantial amount of fluidity in certain counties may be traced to electorate replacement and population growth through migration. On the other hand, it is not possible to account for all or even a major portion of fluidity in this manner. Changes in the residence patterns associated with social class have been evenly balanced during the past three decades, for example, yet low social class is the principal indicator of both high fluidity and high levels of support for Peronism.

In other words, the Peronists' electoral districts also appear to be those with the most fluid electorate, a hypothesis that calls into question the loyalty of the Peronist masses. These districts consistently demonstrated a relatively strong deviation from Perón's directives: when *El líder* called for blank ballots, more than an average number of electors voted for other parties; when he endorsed one of two or more Peronist groups, more than an average number supported the dissident party on election day. If, as these data suggest, Perón had trouble maintaining the rank and file's obedience, his successors will need a nearly superhuman amount of elite consensus to prevent defections and, perhaps, fragmentation of the entire Peronist movement.

It is also interesting to note in both Tables 4.8 and 4.9 that most of the indicators associated with low fluidity have become increasingly related to low Peronist support over time. This supports the common assumption that the anti-Peronist electorate is more consistent in its electoral preferences and suggests further problems for Peronism in the absence of Perón's leadership when electoral activity is resumed.

CONCLUSION

A general picture emerges from this analysis of Peronist electoral behavior: Peronism is a working-class movement with significant middle-class support; it flourishes in places undergoing rapid economic change, which is usually accompanied by significant demographic instability; it is a fluid movement—in contrast to other Argentine political parties, it is subject to a disproportionate amount of voter defection. Most important, Peronism is a popular political movement. Given the opportunity to select its own leadership in free, competitive elections, since 1946 the Argentine people have opted consistently for the Peronist alternative.

But now Perón is dead. His death in mid-1974 occurred ten months after the last national election in Argentina, and so there are no electoral data with which to estimate the strength of Peronism without Perón. If we accept the rational-voter model of electoral behavior, then the types of people who supported Perón in 1973 should still support the Peronist movement in the 1980s. But as the world observed the extraordinary actions of the Argentine government in its seizure of the Malvinas Islands in 1982, it probably recognized that calculations of "rationality" in Argentina might elsewhere be judged irrational.

Thus it would be foolhardy for an outside observer to use pre-1973 data to predict Argentine political behavior in the 1980s. All that is certain is that the Peronist movement will fragment, each part claiming to represent the authentic ideals of *El líder*. Peronism will be as little able to lead the nation as Radicalism was following the death of Yrigoyen. And, like Radicalism, the success of Peronism will therefore come to depend largely upon the behavior of the opposition. This conclusion speculates upon the direction in which the opposition might push Peronism.

THE POSTWAR LIBERAL COALITION

The forces that ousted the Peronist national populist governments in 1955 and 1976 were the vestigial remains of the powerful liberal consensus that dominated Argentina from the fall of Rosas to the passage of the Sáenz Peña Law. Since passage of that legislation nearly sixty years ago, Argentina's liberals have been unable to convince a plurality of the citizenry to favor them at the polls. As a result, liberalism has triumphed only on those occasions (1930, 1955, 1976) when the populist coalition has fractured to the point that liberals, who base their power on coercion, have been encouraged to replace popularity as the means of selecting governments. Without the populists' internal fissures and the liberals' ability to organize the physical intimidation of their rivals, the Argentine liberals probably would have passed from the political scene long ago. There is no evidence to suggest that populists have resolved their internal divisions, however—indeed they will certainly be more pronounced now that Perón is dead—nor does it seem that the liberals' organizational skills are diminishing, and until either or both of these events occur, the liberals will continue to form one of the two crucial coalitions in Argentine politics.

Like the national populists, the liberal coalition is composed of core groups and other actors who enter and leave the coalition as contemporary problems and their political instincts indicate. At the core of the coalition are two groups identified by O'Donnell as major domestic capitalists ("la gran burguesía doméstica") and international capitalists.[1] The former are primarily involved in traditional economic activities—the production and export of agricultural commodities and the operation of manufacturing firms and financial groups that service the primary sector. The latter are the directors of transnational corporations, particularly the international banking community. In the United States, David Rockefeller has championed the cause of Argentine liberalism with extraordinary vigor, and the interest group he founded, the Council of the Americas, has lobbied hard to acquaint both U.S. foreign policymakers and potential investors with the salutary effects of liberal rule in Argentina.

The additional actors in the liberal coalition include the hierarchy of the Argentine church, the armed forces, and a large but extremely varied part of the middle class. It is of considerable importance to emphasize, however, that these actors are themselves internally divided. While military leaders can be counted on to sympathize with the liberal perspective in times of political and economic instability, for example, a significant part of the armed forces views liberalism as a form of *entreguismo* (sell-out to foreign interests) and therefore a threat to Argentina's national security. As Mallon and Sourrouille indicate, the military contribution to the liberal coalition is often contradictory—in the 1930s the military approved the quintessentially liberal Roca-Runciman treaty while encouraging antiliberal exchange controls, increasing export duties, generalizing bilateral trade agreements, and instituting a fairly progressive income tax.[2] Similarly, in the late 1960s and 1970s the Church was sorely fractured over the issue of clergy activism. In May 1970, for example, the Movement of Third World Priests issued a declaration calling for "formal rejection of the present capitalist system" and "socialization of the means of production." In early December 1972, all priests in the archdiocese of Buenos Aires were prohibited from participating in political parties, whereupon the next day seventy of the Third World Priests met with Juan Perón and issued a declaration supporting "the Argentine people's desire for liberation and justice . . . through the Peronist movement." But despite these internal schisms, the leadership of the armed forces and the church can be counted upon to side with the liberals in any *fundamental* confrontation with the populists.

These confrontations generally arise when the national populist coalition is in the process of disintegration, and the society as a result is facing economic and political confusion. In reaction, the coalition of core liberals expands into what O'Donnell has termed a "defensive alliance."[3] One such alliance was formed in 1955, according to David Rock.

> At the time of the military rebellion led by General Eduardo Lonardi in September, 1955, Peronism was on the verge of bankruptcy. It was violently opposed by key power groups like the armed forces and the Church. It was held in odium by the traditional political elites, the commercial bourgeoisie of Buenos Aires, the pampas farming interests, and also by the newer and increasingly powerful industrial interests. Among the middle classes only a small number of groups tied to Perón by the umbilical cord of state patronage lamented his downfall. Also its key area of support among the urban working class had been palpably sagging for some time.[4]

With only slight modification, this statement would describe accurately the period 1974–76 as well.

Once the confrontation with populism is over, however, and the liberals are in power, there is the natural tendency of a fairly heterogeneous coalition to fragment. Disunity is fostered by such intractable issues as taxation, the timing and extent of devaluations that benefit some liberal coalition members while penalizing others, and access to credit and government subsidies. Even the industrialists tend to split, with the supporters of foreign capital challenging the protectionist policies of national entrepreneurs.

Despite these divisions, unity is easier to achieve among liberals than among the national populists because liberals enter public office not in a time of public optimism but rather when the country is in a state of siege. Their backs to the wall, the liberals close ranks and concentrate upon the external enemy, the national populists. The post-1955 liberal government is an excellent example. The first chieftain of the Revolución Libertadora adopted as his administration's slogan the phrase used by Urquiza following the defeat of Rosas in 1852, *ni vencedores ni vencidos*, and promptly attempted to assuage the fear of economic reprisals in the mind of the working class: "Let our working brothers know," he insisted, "that we commit our honor as soldiers in the solemn promise that we will never permit their rights to be curtailed." Within two months, General Lonardi was hastily removed from office after a vain effort to pursue just such a conciliatory policy, and the Argentine workers began to experience the economic repercussions of liberal policy decisions. The amount of gross domestic income paid as wages had risen from about 42 percent in 1940 to 50 percent and more under Perón, but soon plummeted to prewar levels as liberal economists sought to increase entrepreneurial incentives by reconcentrating the wealth Perón had begun to distribute.[5] The cost of living began an incredible continuous upward spiral, as the index based at 100 in 1960 spurted to 1200 by early 1972.[6] Inflation had also plagued Perón's previous administration, but never as severely and, importantly, never with similarly detrimental effects upon the purchasing power of the lower and lower-middle classes, for wage increases had often matched and occasionally outstripped the inexorable rise in prices. Aramburu's economic policy, conversely, was designed to purge the economy of Peronist "excesses" while obtaining the support of Argentina's rural, industrial, and financial groups, as well as the nation's traditional trading partners.[7]

In addition to these financial deprivations, the Aramburu government took a variety of steps to destroy the institutions through which members of the populist coalition influenced politics. The Peronist party, the General Confederation of Labor, and the General Economic Confederation were intervened or disbanded. The all-important Law of Professional Associations (which provided for union strength by specifying that only one union could represent a single economic activity, by banning open shops, and by making employers responsible for collecting union dues) was repealed, the right to strike was severely restricted, and the police were encouraged to take stern action against labor demonstrations. After 1955 the Peronist policy of blanket wage adjustments was replaced by factory-level labor-management bargaining, which had the effect of widening wage differentials and encouraging the creation of a labor aristocracy. Each of these actions suggested a return to a class-based political struggle in which an isolated working class faced industrial and agricultural interests, the army, and the church.[8]

It is possible to argue that Peronism survived in Argentina after 1955 because it was so pointedly persecuted by the liberal coalition. During this period the roles were reversed, as the national populists found their backs against the wall, battling not for political advantage but for political survival in a struggle that appeared to be a war of extermination. In 1956 the summary execution of General Juan José Valle and twenty-six other pro-Peronist military officers following an abortive coup confirmed the worst suspicions of the persecuted. The memoirs of people who had worked with the national populists contain a uniform tone of outrage at the revenge of the liberals. (Perón's minister of war, Franklin Lucero, wrote *El precio de la lealtad* [The price of loyalty]; Perón's labor advisor, José Figuerola, entitled his book *¡Preso!* [Prisoner!]; and Raúl Puigbó wrote *La revancha oligárquica y el porvenir obrero* [The oligarchy's revenge and the workers' future].) The future of which Puigbó wrote included reorganization, resistance, and then revenge. In short, the ouster of Perón in 1955 was followed by a period of political persecution, during which the once-fractured Peronist coalition learned to survive under conditions of extreme adversity.

Had the liberals been content to remove Perón rather than terminate working-class political participation, it is likely that the past quarter-century of Argentine history could have been written much differently. Since this is so obvious to even the casual observer, the Argentine liberals must have been attempting something more than the removal of a single government. Perón had galvanized a political force that had been slowly developing since the founding of the UCR, a political force that could easily outvote any liberal coalition, and which once in power moved to renovate the Argentine structure of privilege. As Luna has written of the Peronist rural laborers' law:

Neither the predicted costs nor the required working conditions modified too much those that previously existed and that were in general humane and reasonable. . . . But [the law's provisions] attacked the bases of traditional rural labor and modified the relationship of dependence of the *peón* with respect to his *patrón*. They closed the paternalistic style of rural work and stipulated the rights and duties of each party in concrete articles, regulating legally what had been until then only determined by the good will of the *patrón*. This was the inadmissible thing, that which created an unacceptable precedent for all those owners who viewed their *estancias* as an exclusive and impregnable place where only the owner's orders were listened to. The dangerous thing was not the salary raises but rather the new concept that now was fastened in the mind of the *peón*: that above the will of the *patrón*, before all-inclusive, there now existed a superior will that was protecting him.[9]

After the fall of Perón in 1955, Argentina's *peones* had to be returned to their proper station in life. This required not only a series of harsh economic measures but also the dismantling of the institutions through which the working class had expressed itself politically. The net impact of the Revolución Libertadora was to deprive the electoral majority of its participatory status in Argentine politics.

However determined the liberals may have been in their desire to regain firm control of Argentine politics, they have been sufficiently realistic to understand that they cannot overcome the bias of the twentieth century in favor of broad political participation. After 1955 they attempted to drive the national populists into non-Peronist political parties, a tactic that worked fairly well once—in 1958—but only until the Peronists were allowed to field their own candidates (for provincial governors in 1962). There then ensued what O'Donnell has labeled the "impossible game," a charade in which the army would announce elections with the hope that some centrist party would attract the national populist working class.[10] First, however, the centrists had to be elected, and so they had to negotiate with Perón for the votes he controlled, just as Frondizi had to solicit Perón's support in order to win the 1958 election. Upon learning of these negotiations, the army stopped the game.

Finally, after every alternative had been explored, in 1970 the liberals admitted to their inability to govern without popular support and arranged for direct political participation by the Peronists. Through the use of a system of ballotage, liberals thought they could prevent a Peronist electoral victory while permitting them sufficient minority representation to lend legitimacy to the political system. The ploy failed, of course, and in mid-1973 the Peronists once again assumed control of the government. Given a choice, Argentine voters once more demonstrated their preference for populism.

It is important to emphasize again that the populist coalition that formed around the candidacy of Héctor Cámpora consisted of more than the working class. One group—the nationalists—merits special consideration, for in the 1980s it may meld with local entrepreneurs to form a solid opposition to the liberal economic policies of post-1976 governments. To underestimate the strength of nationalism as a motivating force is seriously to misinterpret Argentine policies.

Such a misinterpretation is encouraged by Argentina's strong commercial and intellectual ties to Western Europe and the United States, which have contributed to make Argentina the most cosmopolitan nation in Latin America, with Buenos Aires's French and English architecture, Italian cuisine, and North American cinema only as external examples of the *porteños'* tendency to consume the best and worst of foreign cultures. Many thoughtful Argentines have expressed the fear that these intrusions by foreign cultures might bring negative consequences for the nation's collective conscience. The dean of *criollo* nationalism, Ricardo Rojas, wrote as early as 1909 in *La restauración nacionalista* that the invasion of foreign influences threatened to obliterate Argentina's native traditions. By 1922, Rojas appeared resigned to such an eventuality when, in the final volume of *La literatura moderna*, he noted the omnipresence of imported styles and mannerisms and admitted that his nation had been overwhelmed.

Although Rojas was probably the greatest precursor of what has come to be termed Argentine cultural nationalism, he could not be considered antiforeign in the sense the word is used today, for he conceded the necessity of Argentina's substantial links to the Western world. The fact that Argentina pursued economic development with the very substantial assistance of foreign capital and technology, and that this implied a position of subordination to the world's centers of capital, became the major preoccupation of other Argentine nationalists. By the beginning of the Great Depression a new type of nationalism based upon economic and political foundations had begun to take form, a nationalism that stressed the needs for reduced economic dependence and for greater national control of foreign economic inputs. During the decade of the 1930s a number of nationalist political groups were formed with the purpose of reasserting Argentina's cultural, economic, and political independence. Among the most successful of these groups was the Radical Youth Orienting Force (Fuerza Orientadora Radical de la Joven Argentina—FORJA), which originated in mid-1935, first as an internal faction of the UCR and after 1940 as a separate political group. In addition to acting as the primary opposition to the UCR's Alvearist politicians, FORJA's leaders—Arturo Jauretche, Raúl Scalabrini Ortiz, Luis Dellepiane, Gabriel del Mazo, Homero Manzi —composed the intellectual and political core of Argentine nationalism. After the group dissolved in 1945, a number of FORJA members became active participants in Perón's first administration.

When the liberals once again seized power in 1955, they proceeded to create the perception that Argentina would return to the pre-Peronist era of free trade and free access to Argentina's markets. That Perón had already started down this well-worn path was overlooked by most Argentine nationalists, and the criticisms of liberal economic policies were couched in language usually reserved for the discussion of treason. Typical was the work of Arturo Jauretche, whose *El plan Prebisch: retorno al coloniaje* was regularly reissued and updated to include the sins of the latest liberal economic team. *El retorno al coloniaje: la secunda década infame, de Prebisch a Krieger Vasena* (1969) is the masterpiece of its genre, a captivating defense of national industry and government intervention in international trade relations. Other national populists constantly drew the picture of Argentine politics as one in which the Peronists defended national sovereignty and the liberals sold the country's future to foreign capitalists and United States imperialists. Witness the memoirs of Perón's minister of the navy, Rear Admiral Aníbal Olivieri, who in 1958 explained his view of Peronism as the only defense against foreign domination. Of the intervention by Spruille Braden in the 1945–46 election campaign, he wrote: "[Braden] damaged my sensibilities just as he would have damaged those of the North Americans, the Indonesians, or the French if a foreigner took similar liberties against the rights and respect that free people deserve. I decided to support Colonel Perón. I would have supported any Argentine who adopted the position Perón did. If the other presidential candidates also would have rejected that interference, perhaps fate would have maintained me aloof from the open struggle, but he was the only one who did."[11]

If in the 1980s a new populist coalition launches a serious attack upon the reigning liberals, one part of that coalition will surely consist of nationalists who are disturbed by what they consider the *entreguista* policies of José Martínez de Hoz and his successors.

One of Perón's "three flags of *justicialismo*" was economic independence. By this he meant much more than buying foreign holdings in Argentina with the nation's war earnings.[12] Despite occasional deviations, Peronism has generally stood for policies that encourage a self-reliant economy based upon domestic production for domestic markets. No Argentine government will ever be able to ignore completely the nation's place in contemporary world markets—Argentina's current comparative advantage in agriculture is too obvious to be overlooked—but the essential question has never been whether to produce for export; rather it is how to exploit this comparative advantage for the long-term development of the nation.

This debate naturally hinges upon one's view of a desirable future. The liberals appear to favor a future in which Argentina maximizes its existing comparative advantages while permitting other nations with different comparative advantages to have free access to Argentine markets. The populists, conversely, favor the exploitation of the nation's existing comparative advantages to create new economic activities that service the domestic market and that may, over time, create a new comparative advantage and, ipso facto, a more dynamic economy that, because of its diversification, is less subject to the detrimental aspects of changes in world trading conditions for a handful of agricultural products.

As we have seen, when given a chance to select between these two views of Argentina's economic future, Argentines regularly endorse the populist alternative. When this occurs, liberals at home and abroad typically react by lamenting the Argentine electorate's lack of understanding of what are said to be economic laws. To direct scarce resources into areas other than those favored by current comparative advantage is wasteful, they assert. National populists respond that comparative advantages are subject to purposeful change. They note, for example, that until recently the comparative advantage of California's Santa Clara Valley was in growing grapes, but that it is now called Silicon Valley. Similarly, Tiajuana's role in the international economy was as a site for behavior that Californians found unacceptable in their own neighborhoods; now Tiajuana is a center for labor-intensive light manufacturing. Had the United States followed the liberals' advice two centuries ago, the South's principal economic activity would still be the production of cotton for British textile mills. To Argentina's national populists, occasionally it may be desirable to violate what once was viewed as an entirely appropriate economic law.

There is always a gap between what is economically desirable and what is feasible, however, and Argentina's national populists have been unable to produce an economic performance that is acceptable to all major members of the populist coalition. As O'Donnell has indicated, any coalition that includes the urban bourgeoisie and the popular sector contains a built-in instability, and this instability is increased whenever additional actors are added to the coalition and economic deterioration precludes state-controlled class harmony.[13] Both of these features were present in Argentina in the 1970s, and both contributed to the decline and overthrow of populism. Should the populists return to power in the 1980s, the same dilemmas will have to be confronted. There is no evidence whatsoever that the confrontations will produce an acceptable result for the Argentine people.

In the most fundamental way, then, Argentine politics have changed very little during the twentieth century. The Radical intransigence of Hipólito Yrigoyen is today represented by the Peronist movement; the *unicato* of Juárez Celman has been superseded by the liberal elite and its minatory guard, personified in the 1976–80 period by José Martínez de Hoz and Jorge Rafael Videla, respectively. There remains at the very heart of Argentine politics the liberal-populist cleavage, and no foreseeable scenario will replace for any significant period the animosity and mutual distrust these two groups have for each other. Convinced that Peronism would emerge victorious from any electoral contest, the liberals appear determined to control the government indefinitely, permitting gradually expanding participation but never so much as to threaten the basic liberal policies instituted since 1976. In the meantime, buffeted by forces largely beyond its leaders' control, the fragile Argentine economy faces challenges that perhaps no agricultural, export-dependent, semi-industrialized nation can overcome.

If history is any guide, economic crises will eventually force a crisis of legitimacy, and that will lead in turn to the liberals' temporary abandonment of power. Once more a populist coalition, this time without Perón, will attempt to manage the unmanageable, and then the military will once more intervene to establish order. Eventually some new ingredient will be added to Argentine politics that breaks this cycle, but until that time there is little to suggest that tomorrow will be much different from yesterday or today in Argentina.

The day is long past for discussions of the relative merits of survey and aggregate data. For political scientists studying electoral behavior, survey data are almost invariably better data. The simple fact that the aggregation of individual responses and characteristics notoriously exaggerates subsequent correlation coefficients causes even the most brazen political scientists to tread warily, if at all, through the treacherous morass of aggregate data.

As early as 1934, Charles Elmer Gehkle and Katherine Biehel called this inflationary tendency to their colleagues' attention with a vivid description of the effects of aggregation in an analysis of the relationship between delinquency and property values in 252 Cleveland census tracts. Progressively grouping contiguous areas, they managed to raise the Pearson correlation from $-.502$ to $-.763$.[1] By 1950, G. Udny Yule and Maurice G. Kendall had demonstrated that a similar aggregation of forty-eight English counties skyrocketed the somewhat less than intriguing correlation between wheat and potato yields from .219 to .765, and concluded that "on the face of it we seem able to produce any value of the correlation from 0 to 1 by choosing an appropriate size of area for which we measure the yields."[2]

That same vintage year for methodological iconoclasts saw the publication of William Robinson's justly famous attempt to indicate the specific potential for distortion inherent in making individual inferences from aggregate data. His most stunning example compared the individual correlation between race and literacy (.203) to the same United States Census aggregate correlation (.946).[3] The statistical origin of this remarkable phenomenon is to be found in the fact that

> the individual correlation depends upon the *internal* frequencies of the within-areas individual correlations, while the ecological correlation depends upon the *marginal* frequencies of the within-areas individual correlations. Moreover, it is well-known that the marginal frequencies of a fourfold table do not determine the internal frequencies. There is a large number of sets of internal frequencies which will satisfy ex-

actly the same marginal frequencies for any fourfold table. . . . In short, the within-areas marginal frequencies which determine the percentages from which the ecological correlation is computed do not fix the internal frequencies which determine the individual correlation. *Thus there need be no correspondence between the individual correlation and the ecological correlation.*[4]

After indicating in addition that the net effect of consolidation is to increase the numerical value of the ecological correlation, Robinson concluded that "the relation between ecological and individual correlations which is discussed in this paper provides a definite answer as to whether ecological correlations can validly be used as substitutes for individual correlations. They cannot."[5]

A number of respected scholars have attempted unsuccessfully to modify Robinson's assertion. W. Phillips Shively gathered together and expanded upon several efforts to reduce the bias inherent in the aggregation of individual characteristics, but others stubbornly refused to face the issue squarely. Austin Ranney, for example, insisted that "if aggregate data studies carefully and thoroughly identify and describe recurring patterns of preference and turnout characteristic of particular electorates over time and, by ecological correlations, relate those patterns to other traits of the electorates and their environments, they can be valuable allies to the sample surveys in the investigation of electoral behavior."[6] But this is true only if the criterion of aggregation is of theoretical import. If anarchists or blue-collar workers or rural migrants were to be grouped discretely, the problem of aggregation would cease to exist for these categories. Unfortunately, of course, this is rarely the case, for analysts of aggregate electoral behavior rely upon theoretically neutral *areal* aggregation—census tracts, electoral precincts, and the larger units into which they in turn are consolidated. This accidental aggregation of voters can never adequately replace individual-level responses and properties in the analysis of electoral behavior.

If aggregate data are to be "valuable allies to the sample surveys in the investigation of electoral behavior," one must take advantage of their most prominent assets—availability and low cost—and employ them as initial data bases for exploratory studies. Aggregate data can frequently and admirably indicate variables that merit further investigation and aid in the formulation of testable hypotheses. Then the consequences of arriving at erroneous conclusions are far outweighed by the opportunities to raise provocative questions. That is the approach used in the present study.[7]

The electoral data are, first, for all 209 *circuitos*, or precincts, in the Federal Capital (Buenos Aires) between 1942 and 1973. They were obtained from the Secretaría Electoral de la Capital Federal. With the exception of the data for 1957 and 1973, all of the electoral data from the Federal Capital were calculated by adding the vote of every party for every *mesa* of every *circuito* in eight elections between 1942 and 1973. The number of parties varied from 2 to 26, and the number of *mesas* from 3500 to more than 7000. Electoral personnel aggregated the 1957 and 1973 data to the *circuito* level.

The 39 units of Greater Buenos Aires make up the second data set used in this volume. This is the sum of the Federal Capital's 20 *secciones*, or wards, and the 19 *partidos*, or counties, which together with the River Plate surround the Federal Capital. (Two terms are employed to indicate the Argentine equivalent of a United States county. The province of Buenos Aires alone retains a semblance of Hispanic purity by the use of *partido*; elsewhere in this land of Francophiles only *departamento* is officially acceptable. The Federal Capital's *secciones* are commonly referred to as *circunscripciones*.) While interesting because of the large number of variables available for analysis, the units themselves vary considerably in size and are much larger than the Federal Capital's precincts.

The third data set comprises all the 504 *departamentos* in Argentina outside Greater Buenos Aires. Although these differ enormously, most counties are heterogeneous units with urban county seats and substantial rural acreage. The electoral data were supplied by the Dirección Nacional Electoral, and should be accurate. As pointed out periodically in the preceding chapters, however, there is reason to believe that when working with the returns from several very rural counties (especially those where more than 125 percent of the registered voters vote) a healthy skepticism is an analytic necessity. The elections being examined took place over a period of more than thirty years. During that time a number of boundary changes occurred, and so the number of cases must vary slightly. So long as the variation is not too great and the reader is aware that the data are from somewhat different populations, this poses no problem when analyzing simple zero-order correlation coefficients. When working with the partial coefficients upon which multiple regression analyses are based, however, it is imperative that zero-order coefficients be computed from the same universe. In some cases the net effect of this requirement is to reduce the workable *N* from nearly 500 to as low as 220.

Each of the eight elections was unique. The 1946 presidential election is studied in each of the data sets. By the time of the 1951 presidential election, however, Argentina had temporarily switched to single-member districts unrelated to county boundaries, and so only votes in the Federal Capital's unchanged precincts are appropriate for analysis. As a surrogate, the 1954 congressional elections are utilized for Greater Buenos Aires. Following the 1955 Revolución Libertadora, isolation of the Peronist vote becomes impossible at times. For this reason the 1958 presidential election (in which the Peronists were ordered to vote for Arturo Frondizi, the candidate of one of the UCR's two principal factions, the Unión Cívica Radical Intransigente) and the 1963 presidential election (in which many Peronists joined *frondizistas* and other small groups in casting blank ballots) are excluded. All blank ballots cast in the 1957 special election for delegates to a constitutional convention are considered Peronist, as are the blank ballots cast in the 1960 election for members of the Chamber of Deputies. It is widely believed that many Peronists broke party discipline and voted for one candidate or another in both elections, but while a certain portion of the non-Peronist electorate also cast blank ballots (particularly the Communists in 1957), the overwhelming majority of blank ballots in 1957 and 1960 was Peronist. In elections for representatives to the Chamber of Deputies in 1962 and 1965, Peronists sought office under the banner of the Unión Popular. In 1962 the picture is complicated by the fact that the very small Partido Socialista Argentino de Vanguardia supported Peronist candidates in the Federal Capital and that the neo-Peronist Partido Tres Banderas dropped out of the contest in the Federal Capital two days prior to the election but after its ballots had become available. In 1965 two minor parties (the Alianza de la Justicia Social and the Movimiento Las Flores-Luján) supported candidates of the Peronist Unión Popular. Finally, the September 1973 election was the one in which Juan Perón once more captured the Argentine presidency. As of mid-1982, it was the last national election held in Argentina.

Outside Greater Buenos Aires data are from the 1946 presidential election, the 1954 congressional election, the 1957 constitutional convention election, and the 1960, 1962, and 1965 congressional elections. While it is commonly agreed that blank ballots indicate the Peronist vote in 1957 and 1960, it is doubtful whether agreement will ever be reached on a definitive list of Peronist parties for 1962 and 1965. Nevertheless, votes for the following parties represent a fairly accurate estimate of Peronism's electoral strength in 1962: Unión Popular (Federal Capital and Buenos Aires province), Partido Populista (Catamarca, Corrientes, Chubut, Santa Cruz), Partido Laborista (Córdoba, Jujuy, La Pampa, Santa Fe, Tucumán), Movimiento Cívico Bandera Popular (Chaco), Partido de la Provincia de Chubut (Chubut), Partido Tres Banderas (Entre Ríos, Mendoza, Santa Fe, Santiago del Estero), Partido Blanco (Mendoza, Río Negro), Partido Justicialista (Misiones), Movimiento Popular Neuquino (Neuquén), Partido Laborista Nacional (Salta). Peronist votes were indistinguishable from those of other parties with whom alliances were formed in Formosa, La Rioja (both with the Partido Demócrata Cristiano), San Juan (UCR Bloquista), and San Luis (Partido Demócrata Liberal). Five provinces held their elections before the 18 March general election date: Catamarca, Santa Fe, and San Luis (all on 17 December 1961), Formosa (14 January 1962), and La Rioja (25 February 1962).

The 1965 Peronist parties are the following: Unión Popular (Federal Capital, Buenos Aires, Catamarca, Córdoba, Corrientes, Chaco, Chubut, Entre Ríos, Formosa, La Pampa, La Rioja, Mendoza, Misiones, Salta, San Juan, San Luis, Santa Cruz, Santa Fe, Santiago del Estero, Tucumán), Partido Tres Banderas (Entre Ríos, Santiago del Estero), Movimiento Popular Mendocino (Mendoza), Movimiento Popular Neuquino (Neuquén), Partido Justicialista (Salta, Mendoza), Partido Laborista (Salta), Partido Blanco (Río Negro, Salta, Santa Fe), Acción Provinciana (Tucumán), Partido de la Justicia Social (Buenos Aires), Movimiento Las Flores-Luján (Buenos Aires), Unión Provincial (Misiones), Movimiento de la Justicia Social (Misiones). There were no elections in Jujuy. In 1963 the newly elected members of the Chamber of Deputies drew lots to determine which half would have two-year and which half would have normal four-year terms in office. Five provinces (Catamarca, Formosa, La Rioja, Misiones, and Salta) had deputies who all drew four-year terms, and so their 1965 election results are for provincial deputies.

The composite dependent variable PERON is utilized to simplify data presentation. The first step in the construction of PERON was to factor analyze the seven dependent variables representing the percentage vote for Peronism in 1946, 1951 (or 1954), 1957, 1960, 1962, 1965, and 1973. Using the single factor score coefficient matrix produced by the analysis, the composite variable PERON was computed by summing the products of each variable's standardized score and its factor score coefficient (see Table A1). Table A2 contains the simple Pearson correlations between PERON and the Peronist vote in the separate elections in the Federal Capital and Greater Buenos Aires.

SOCIOECONOMIC VARIABLES

The independent socioeconomic variables have also been separated into three distinct data sets.

The precinct-level data from the Federal Capital refer only to social class as measured by occupation. I believe they are the most reliable data available for use in the ecological analysis of Argentine electoral behavior. These data were obtained from a 10 percent random-start, fixed-interval sample of registration forms for all male voters as of October 1959. Then, using the same precinct tables (*mesas*) sampled in 1959, a further 10 percent sample was made of the 1945 voter registration lists (that is, 10 percent of the 1959 10 percent) and very few changes in the occupational structure of the Federal Capital's precincts were found to have occurred

TABLE A1

Factor Score Coefficients and Component Variables of PERON

Component Variable (percentage vote for Peronism)	Factor Score	Mean	Standard Deviation
1946	.14	55.8	8.27
1954	.15	59.2	8.64
1957	.15	22.1	6.97
1960	.15	25.9	7.76
1962	.15	32.3	9.94
1965	.15	38.6	8.77
1973	.15	58.4	13.22

TABLE A2

Pearson Correlations between PERON
and Its Component Variables

	PERON	
	---	---
Election	Greater Buenos Aires ($N=37$)	Federal Capital ($N=209$)
1946	.89	.90
1951 (1954)	.97	.95
1957	.97	.95
1960	.96	.96
1962	.99	.92
1965	.98	.97
1973	.96	.93

during the intervening fourteen years. Working-class areas, in particular, maintained an extremely stable class structure. Ezequiel Martínez Estrada noted long ago that the class ecology of Buenos Aires had adopted its fundamental outlines by the turn of the century.[8]

In Argentina male voter registration is tied to registration for military service, and a very severe sanction (up to an extra year of military duty) is imposed upon those who fail to register within three months of their eighteenth birthday. Because they exclude so few males, the registration lists provide an unusually accurate estimate of a precinct's occupational structure.[9] It is impossible to obtain a stratified female sample. More than 50 percent of registered females are classified as housewives or unemployed, and a large majority of the remainder apparently is engaged in some aspect of dressmaking. This activity is subdivided into as many as thirty processes, each claiming a rather ambiguous rank on a nearly incoherent occupational pecking order.

With the assistance of more than a dozen employees of the Secretaría Electoral and several Argentine and United States social scientists living in Buenos Aires, six occupational categories were rank-ordered according to contemporary Argentine standards of social stratification. Of highest status is the "professional" category —attorneys, doctors, engineers, owners or managers of large enterprises, persons supported by their investments, and so forth. Argentine professionals appear to occupy the same relative social position as the upper middle class in the United States. No attempt was made to identify the upper class; presumably its members are included in the data as professionals. Next in social status are students. Given the orientations of Argentina's universities, students who pursue their studies until graduation become professionals. For this reason it is not surprising that the ecological correlation between percent professionals and percent students is +.65. Businessmen are third on the scale. This is an extremely vague category for all types of middle-class men who are self-employed in the broadest possible sense. Readers familiar with the varied use of *comerciante* will appreciate the imprecision of this category. Fortunately, there are relatively few self-declared businessmen in Buenos Aires; in no precinct are they more than 9 percent of the registered male population, and the mean is slightly less than 5 percent. "Employees" are white-collar workers, "workers" are blue-collar workers, and "unskilled workers" are *peones*.

Treatment of the independent variables in the second data set, that of Greater Buenos Aires, proved infinitely more difficult. The fundamental problem is multicollinearity: several of the *conceptually distinct* variables tend to vary together. This is only natural, of course, for economic change can hardly occur without demographic instability or industrialization. Nor is the population density of the zones of temporary huts that harbor large numbers of urban working-class citizens equal to that of the zones of middle- and upper-class high-rise apartment complexes, for flat terrain and relatively efficient mass transportation encourage extensive rather than intensive land use by the Buenos Aires working class.

As expected, therefore, an initial factor analysis of the twenty-six variables employed in this study yielded five rather unclear orthogonal factors (see Table A3). Because the factors appeared so difficult to interpret and, more important, because this was to be a test of hypotheses from a variety of previous analyses, the factors in Table A3 were bypassed and the variables were separated into six groups (WORKING CLASS, POPULATION GROWTH, URBANIZATION, SATISFACTION, INDUSTRY, and INDUSTRIAL GROWTH) according to prior usage. When prior usage proved inconsistent among various authors, decisions were made by appealing to political science's ever-ambiguous court of last resort, common sense. No reader will agree with all of the groupings, although some (particularly WORK-

ING CLASS, POPULATION GROWTH, and INDUSTRIAL GROWTH) will be far less controversial than others.

Factor analyses then explored the relationships between the composite groups. Results included verification of the differences that underlie the separation of POPULATION GROWTH and URBANIZATION (see Table A4). Internally, the six groups were considered relatively homogeneous when principal factoring without iteration produced only one factor with an eigenvalue greater than unity. Then the six composite variables were constructed in the same manner as PERON, by summing the products of each variable's standardized score and its factor score coefficient.

At this point the problem of multicollinearity between WORKING CLASS, POPULATION GROWTH, URBANIZATION, and INDUSTRIAL GROWTH became acute. The zero-order Pearson correlation between WORKING CLASS and POPULATION GROWTH was +.71; between WORKING CLASS and URBANIZATION it was −.79; and between POPULATION GROWTH and INDUSTRIAL GROWTH it was +.79. These correlations would make several partial correlations with PERON all but meaningless, and so factor analysis was employed once more, this time using only the thirteen variables grouped into WORKING CLASS, POPULATION GROWTH, URBANIZATION, and INDUSTRIAL GROWTH. The results of an orthogonal analysis were disappointing, but an oblique (oblimin) rotation produced three distinct factors that could be clearly labeled WORKING CLASS, POPULATION GROWTH, and URBANIZATION. The four INDUSTRIAL GROWTH variables loaded randomly and were eliminated from further factoring. The nine WORKING CLASS, POPULATION GROWTH, and URBANIZATION variables were factored once more with an oblique rotation, and the results are presented in Table A5. Then the composite variables WORKING CLASS, POPULATION GROWTH, and URBANIZATION were recomputed using the newly generated factor score coefficients. By this method the original WORKING CLASS–POPULATION GROWTH correlation of +.71 was reduced to +.35, the WORKING CLASS–URBANIZATION correlation of −.79 to −.16, and the URBANIZATION–POPULATION GROWTH correlation of −.38 to −.30. The redefinition of POPULATION GROWTH led to an increase in the POPULATION GROWTH–INDUSTRIAL GROWTH correlation of +.79 to +.84. The independent variable URBANIZATION was subsequently eliminated from the analysis owing to insufficient variation.

The five composite independent variables were constructed as indicated in Tables A6 through A10. Because each of the twenty-six

TABLE A3

Orthogonally (Varimax) Rotated Factor Matrix
for All Independent Variables

Variables	Factor 1	Factor 2	Factor 3	Factor 4	Factor 5
% Industrial workers[b]					
1947	(.58)[a]	.37	(−.54)	.03	.00
1960	.17	(.78)	−.13	.48	.00
% Illiterates, 1960	.17	.47	−.32	(.63)	.13
% Population growth					
1914–47	−.08	(.87)	−.19	.11	−.23
1947–60	−.15	(.66)	.01	(.61)	.00
Population density increase					
1914–47	−.09	(.87)	−.19	.12	−.23
1947–60	.06	(.72)	−.35	.33	−.11
% Urban population					
1947	.20	−.13	−.03	(−.90)	−.04
1960	.19	−.01	.06	(−.86)	−.01
Wages per industrial employee					
1935	−.07	−.13	(.88)	−.16	.16
1941	.06	(−.51)	(.82)	−.02	−.12
1967	.12	−.28	(.89)	.04	.08
Workers per industrial establishment					
1935	(.81)	−.09	−.09	−.14	.32
1941	(.92)	−.04	−.23	−.10	−.01
1947	(.92)	.06	−.18	−.04	.22
1963	(.63)	−.20	.08	.04	(.63)

Wages per industrial establishment					
1935	(.73)	−.15	.39	−.20	.30
1941	(.90)	−.24	.18	−.12	−.04
1947	(.93)	−.06	.17	−.04	.22
1963	.46	−.06	.20	.03	(.77)
Value of production per industrial establishment					
1947	(.97)	−.01	.03	−.06	.12
1963	(.50)	.02	−.03	.15	(.73)
Increase in industrial establishments					
1914–47	−.10	(.89)	−.16	−.29	−.07
1947–63	−.04	(.80)	−.25	.36	.16
Increase in industrial workers					
1914–47	−.16	(.90)	−.15	−.11	.11
1947–63	−.24	(.68)	−.02	.46	.37
Eigenvalues	6.96	6.85	3.31	3.27	2.19
% Total variation	26.77	26.37	12.75	12.56	8.43
% Common variation	31.06	30.59	14.79	14.57	9.78

Note: Principal factoring without iteration using as the extraction criterion factors with eigenvalues greater than unity.

a. Factor loadings ≥ |.50| shown in parentheses.

b. See Tables A6–A10 for complete variable label.

TABLE A4

Orthogonally (Varimax) Rotated Factor Matrix for Demographic Variables

Variables	Factor 1	Factor 2
Average annual percent population growth		
1914–47	(.97)[a]	−.08
1947–60	(.59)	(−.66)
Average annual change in population density		
1914–47	(.97)	−.08
1947–60	(.84)	−.29
Urban population as a percent of total population		
1947	−.17	(.90)
1960	−.03	(.93)
Eigenvalues	2.96	2.21
% Total variation	49.40	36.78
% Common variation	57.11	42.52

Note: Principal factoring without iteration using as the extraction criterion factors with eigenvalues greater than unity.
a. Factor loadings ≥ |.50| shown in parentheses.

variables is standardized, the factor score coefficients determine the relative impact of each component variable upon the composite variable.

Table A11 contains the first- and second-order partial correlations between PERON and each of the five composite independent variables. Table A12 is an independent composite variable correlation matrix.

TABLE A5

Oblique Primary Factors of Nine Socioeconomic Variables

Variables	Pattern			Structure		
	Factor 1 (POPULATION GROWTH)	Factor 2 (URBANI-ZATION)	Factor 3 (WORKING CLASS)	Factor 1 (POPULATION GROWTH)	Factor 2 (URBANI-ZATION)	Factor 3 (WORKING CLASS)
% Industrial workers[a]						
1947	.06	.22	(.95)	.33	.06	(.93)
1960	(.52)	−.36	.43	(.77)	(−.57)	(.67)
% Illiterates, 1960	.10	(−.51)	(.67)	.48	(−.64)	(.78)
% Population growth						
1914–47	(.99)	.08	.08	(.98)	.21	.34
1947–60	(.51)	(−.60)	.00	(.69)	(−.75)	.28
Population density increase						
1914–47	(.99)	.07	.00	(.97)	−.22	.34
1947–60	(.73)	−.16	.21	(.85)	−.41	.49
% Urban population						
1947	−.10	(.91)	.13	−.32	(.92)	−.05
1960	.13	(.92)	−.04	−.15	(.89)	−.14

Note: Oblimin (δ = −.5) solution. Initial criterion value 5.65, final criterion value 3.64. Loadings and coefficients ≥ |.50| shown in parentheses.

a. See Table A6 for complete variable label.

TABLE A6

Factor Score Coefficients and
Component Variables of WORKING CLASS

Component Variable	Factor Score
Industrial workers as a percent of economically active population	
1947	.630
1960	.225
Illiterates as a percent of total population, 1960	.410
Average annual percent population growth	
1914–47	−.087
1947–60	−.078
Average annual change in population density	
1914–47	−.087
1947–60	.065

TABLE A7

Factor Score Coefficients and
Component Variables of POPULATION GROWTH

Component Variable	Factor Score
Industrial workers as a percent of economically active population	
1947	−.049
1960	.106
Illiterates as a percent of total population, 1960	−.068
Average annual percent population growth	
1914–47	.352
1947–60	.153
Average annual change in population density	
1914–47	.351
1947–60	.223

TABLE A8

Factor Score Coefficients and
Component Variables of SATISFACTION

Component Variable (Wages per industrial employee)	Factor Score
1935	.358
1941	.370
1947	.370

TABLE A9

Factor Score Coefficients and
Component Variables of INDUSTRIAL GROWTH

Component Variable	Factor Score
Average annual increase in industrial establishments	
1941–47	.273
1947–60	.296
Average annual increase in industrial blue-collar workers	
1941–47	.299
1947–60	.270

TABLE A10

Factor Score Coefficients and
Component Variables of INDUSTRY

Component Variable	Factor Score
Blue-collar workers per industrial establishment	
1935	.120
1941	.124
1947	.130
1963	.129
Wages per industrial establishment	
1935	.119
1941	.128
1947	.134
1963	.107
Value of production per industrial establishment	
1947	.129
1963	.097

TABLE A11

Partial Correlations between PERON and the
Composite Independent Variables

	WORKING CLASS	POPULATION GROWTH	SATISFACTION	INDUSTRY	INDUSTRIAL GROWTH
Zero order:					
PERON	.77	.69	−.47	.15	.79
First order controlling for:					
WORKING CLASS		.70	−.11	−.34	.79
POPULATION GROWTH	.77		−.23	.41	.54
SATISFACTION	.69	.60		.21	.72
INDUSTRY	.79	.74	−.49		.84
INDUSTRIAL GROWTH	.77	.08	−.15	.48	
Second order controlling for:					
WORKING CLASS, POPULATION GROWTH			.21	−.06	.53
WORKING CLASS, SATISFACTION		.71		−.33	.81
WORKING CLASS, INDUSTRY		.65	.05		.76
WORKING CLASS, INDUSTRIAL GROWTH		.16	.29	.05	

(Continued on p. 114)

TABLE A11 (*continued*)

	WORKING CLASS	POPULATION GROWTH	SATISFACTION	INDUSTRY	INDUSTRIAL GROWTH
POPULATION GROWTH, SATISFACTION	.77			.41	.51
POPULATION GROWTH, INDUSTRY	.72		−.25		.60
POPULATION GROWTH, INDUSTRIAL GROWTH	.77				
SATISFACTION, INDUSTRY	.71	.67	−.14	.49	.79
SATISFACTION, INDUSTRIAL GROWTH	.78	.07		.49	
INDUSTRY, INDUSTRIAL GROWTH	.68	.15	−.17		

TABLE A12

Independent Composite Variable Product-Moment Correlation Matrix

	WORKING CLASS	POPULATION GROWTH	SATISFACTION	INDUSTRY	INDUSTRIAL GROWTH
WORKING CLASS	1.00	.35	-.54	.45	.43
POPULATION GROWTH		1.00	-.47	-.21	.84
SATISFACTION			1.00	.08	-.50
INDUSTRY				1.00	-.18
INDUSTRIAL GROWTH					1.00

NOTES

CHAPTER 1

1. Shklar, *Men and Citizens*, p. 217. For an informative analysis of the various meanings of "populism," see Tindall, "Populism: A Semantic Identity Crisis."
2. Wiles, "A Syndrome, Not a Doctrine," p. 166; Shils, *The Torment of Secrecy*, pp. 98–104.
3. Worsley, "The Concept of Populism," p. 245.
4. Johnson, "Populism, Reaction, and Revolution in Latin America," pp. 21–22; T. S. Di Tella, "Populism and Reform in Latin America," p. 74.
5. Hennessy, "Latin America," p. 35.
6. Ibid., p. 29.
7. T. S. Di Tella, "Populism and Reform in Latin America," p. 47.
8. Johnson, "Populism, Reaction, and Revolution in Latin America," p. 19; T. S. Di Tella, "Populism and Reform in Latin America," p. 49; Hennessy, "Latin America," p. 31–32; Wiles, "A Syndrome, Not a Doctrine," p. 167; Stewart, "The Social Roots," p. 190; Germani, *Política y sociedad*, p. 212.
9. Johnson, "Populism, Reaction, and Revolution in Latin America," pp. 18–19.
10. T. S. Di Tella, "Ideologías monolíticas," p. 274.
11. T. S. Di Tella, "Populism and Reform in Latin America," p. 50. The widespread existence of status incongruence in Argentina is noted in Sebreli, *Buenos Aires*, p. 63.
12. T. S. Di Tella, "Ideologías monolíticas," p. 273.
13. Hennessy, "Latin America," p. 33; T. S. Di Tella, "Populism and Reform in Latin America," p. 50.
14. T. S. Di Tella, "Populism and Reform in Latin America," pp. 54, 56, 65.
15. Ibid., pp. 55, 57, 64.
16. Martz, *Acción Democrática*, pp. 9–13; Hennessy, "Latin America," p. 28.
17. Prewitt, "Political Socialization and Leadership Selection," p. 109.
18. Deutsch, "Social Mobilization and Political Development," p. 494.
19. Ibid., p. 493.
20. Germani, *Política y sociedad*. See also Smith, "Social Mobilization," pp. 30–49.
21. Germani, *Política y sociedad*, p. 151; Germani, "Mass Society," pp. 586–95.
22. It should be emphasized that there is no inherent reason why traditional political parties cannot adapt to changing circumstances and integrate newly mobilized social sectors. This is particularly true in much of Latin America, where a relatively high level of elite political sophistication and modern government frameworks have often permitted such accommodation. An excellent example is the Colombian party system.

CHAPTER 2

1. World Bank, *World Bank Development Report*, pp. 156–57.
2. Pérez Esquivel was only the second Latin American to be awarded this honor.

The other recipient was also an Argentine, Carlos Saavedra Lamas, who won the prize in 1936 for his efforts to end the Chaco War.

3. Véliz, *The Centralist Tradition of Latin America*, p. 306.

4. Mallon and Sourrouille, *Economic Policymaking in a Conflict Society*, p. 5.

5. Díaz Alejandro, *Essays on the Economic History of the Argentine Republic*, p. 217; Tandy, *Argentina: Economic and Social Conditions in the Argentine Republic*, p. 11.

6. Gallo, *Agrarian Expansion and Industrial Development in Argentina*, pp. 10–11; Dorfman, *Historia de la industria argentina*, pp. 157, 220.

7. Ferrer, *The Argentine Economy*, p. 223; Scobie, *Argentina: A City and a Nation*, p. 182; Fillol, *Social Factors in Economic Development*, p. 45.

8. Quoted in Panettieri, *Síntesis histórica del desarrollo industrial argentino*, p. 74–75.

9. Fayt, *La naturaleza del peronismo*, p. 80; Díaz Alejandro, *Essays on the Economic History of the Argentine Republic*, p. 10; McGann, *Argentina*, p. 43.

10. Dirección General de Estadística, *Anuario estadístico de la República Argentina*, p. 434; Ministerio de Asuntos Técnicos, *IV censo general de la Nación*, p. 52; Germani, *Estructura social de la Argentina*, p. 171; Ferrer, *The Argentine Economy*, p. 165.

11. Germani, "Mass Immigration and Modernization in Argentina," p. 176.

12. Germani, *Estructura social de la Argentina*, p. 174; Ministerio de Hacienda, *Informe demográfico de la Repúblic Argentina*, p. 136.

13. Banco de la Nación, *Encuesta sobre inmigración*, pp. 32–33.

14. Romero, *Breve historia de la Argentina*, p. 86.

15. T. S. Di Tella, *El sistema político argentino y la clase obrera*, p. 10; Germani, *Estructura social de la Argentina*, p. 77.

16. Ministerio de Asuntos Técnicos, *IV censo general de la Nación*, pp. i, lxix.

17. Ingenieros, *Sociología argentina*, p. 68.

18. Rodríguez, *Irigoyen*, p. 84–85; Landenberger and Conte, *Unión Cívica*, p. 151; Snow, *Argentine Radicalism*, pp. 10–11.

19. Landenberger and Conte, *Unión Cívica*, pp. 189–92.

20. del Mazo, *El radicalismo*, p. 134.

21. Mallon and Sourrouille, *Economic Policymaking in a Conflict Society*, p. 56.

22. Snow, *Argentine Radicalism*, p. 35.

23. Quoted in Romero, *Las ideas políticas en la Argentina*, p. 221.

24. Smith, "Social Mobilization, Political Participation, and the Rise of Juan Perór," pp. 48–49.

25. E. Sábato, *El otro rostro del peronismo*, p. 20; de Imaz, *Los que mandan*, p. 208; Cantón, *Party Alignments in Argentina*, p. 11; Melo, *Los partidos políticos argentinos*, pp. 43–44.

26. Rock, "The Survival and Restoration of Peronism," pp. 189–90.

27. Quoted in Peyrou and Villanueva, "Documentos para la historia del peronismo," pp. 212–13.

28. *Filosofía peronista*, pp. 111, 139.

29. The rally occurred on 13 May 1953. Perón was perhaps misinterpreting his late wife's philosophy, for the irreplaceable Evita clearly maintained a very special understanding of social classes. To her, humanity had been divided into three classes: common or mediocre (anti-Peronists), superior (Peronists), and extraordinary (St. Thomas, Rousseau, Confucius, Marx, Alexander the Great, Napoleon, and Juan Perón). Evita's remarkable *Historia del peronismo* is a transcript of the classes she gave beginning in early 1951 as *profesora extraordinaria* at the Escuela Superior Peronista. A few of the chapter headings include: "Christianity and Peronism" and "Other Precursors of Peronism," "Perón Is the Flag of Humanity," "The Greatness of

Perón," "Perón Cannot Be Replaced," "Perón, Example of Humility," "Perón's Humility Is Not Faked," "Perón's Only Defect [he had too much heart]," "Always Love Perón," "With Perón We Will Be Happier," and "Die for Perón." The volume also points out that "Perón is the face of God in the darkness" (p. 46), that the 17th of October was a more important moment in history than the French revolution (p. 61), and that "Perón is Fatherland, Perón is work, Perón is well being, Perón . . . is perfect." Eva Perón, *Historia del peronismo*, pp. 33, 43, 135–36.

30. Quoted in Peyrou and Villanueva, "Documentos para la historia del peronismo," p. 212.

31. Ibid., pp. 214–15, 269–70.

32. Juan Perón, *La hora de los pueblos*, p. 170.

33. Rock, "The Survival and Restoration of Peronism," pp. 187–95.

34. Special care must be taken when comparing these data with those from the 1942 election, for a radical realignment of parties occurred prior to the initial Peronist victory. Virtually all of Argentina's established political parties confirmed Charles Dudley Warner's observation about strange bedfellows by uniting against Perón in the Unión Democrática.

35. Kirkpatrick, *Leader and Vanguard in Mass Society*, p. 94.

36. Ibid., p. 96.

37. Sebreli, *Buenos Aires*, pp. 98, 99, 102–3; T. S. Di Tella, "Populism and Reform in Latin America," pp. 71–72; Carri, *Sindicatos y poder en la Argentina*, p. 61.

38. Kirkpatrick, *Leader and Vanguard in Mass Society*, p. 97. Peter Snow has used aggregate data to confirm the existence of substantial Peronist support in the middle class. See his "Class Basis of Argentine Political Parties," p. 166.

39. Cantón, *El parlamento argentino en épocas de cambio*, p. 12.

40. Snow, *Political Forces in Argentina*, 1st ed., p. 96.

41. Carri, *Sindicatos y poder en la Argentina*, p. 171.

42. Dorfman, *Historia de la industria argentina*, p. 194.

43. Luna, *El 45: crónica de un año decisivo*, p. 86, 373.

44. E. Sábato, *El otro rostro del peronismo*, p. 18.

45. Alexander, *Labor Relations in Argentina, Brazil, and Chile*, pp. 168–69; Carri, *Sindicatos y poder en la Argentina*, p. 25.

46. Melo, *Los partidos políticos argentinos*, p. 70; Departamento Nacional del Trabajo, *Organización sindical*, p. 50; Cerrutti Costa, *El sindicalismo*, pp. 121–22, 131.

47. Departamento Nacional del Trabajo, *Organización sindical*, p. 30.

48. Quoted in Peyrou and Villanueva, "Documentos para la historia del peronismo," p. 253.

49. de Imaz, *Los que mandan*, p. 225; Baily, *Labor, Nationalism, and Politics in Argentina*, p. 70; Fayt, *La naturaleza del peronismo*, p. 90.

50. Consejo Nacional de Postguerra, *Ordenamiento económico-social*, p. 27.

51. Cerrutti Costa, *El sindicalismo*, pp. 124–25.

52. Fayt, *La naturaleza del peronismo*, p. 106.

53. The Consejo Deliberante had been disbanded 10 October 1941 because, according to President Castillo, it had "lost the public's confidence" following revelations that nearly all of its members had accepted bribes to prolong the franchise of the city's foreign-owned electricity company. Ministerio del Interior, *Las fuerzas armadas restituyen el imperio de la soberanía popular*, 1:608.

54. Luna, *El 45: crónica de un año decisivo*, pp. 403–10.

55. Interview with Cipriano Reyes, Buenos Aires, 25 April 1972.

56. de Imaz, *Los que mandan*, p. 5.

57. Worsley, "The Concept of Populism," p. 245.

58. Vaky, "Hemispheric Relations," p. 631.

59. Rock, "The Survival and Restoration of Peronism," p. 215. Aramburu was kidnapped on 29 May 1970, and Onganía was ousted on 8 June, a week before Aramburu's body was found.

60. Canitrot, "La viabilidad económica de la democracia"; Landi, "La tercera presidencia de Perón."

61. James, "The Peronist Left," p. 287.

62. Wynia, *Argentina in the Postwar Era*, pp. 221–22.

CHAPTER 3

1. Deutsch, "Social Mobilization and Political Development," pp. 495, 503.

2. Inkeles, "Participant Citizenship in Six Developing Countries," p. 1138.

3. Nie, Powell, and Prewitt, "Social Structure and Political Participation," pp. 819–21, 825.

4. Cornelius, "The Political Sociology of Cityward Migration in Latin America," pp. 95–147; Cornelius, "Urbanization as an Agent in Latin American Political Instability," p. 833–57.

5. Solberg, "Immigration and Urban Social Problems in Argentina and Chile," p. 232; Butler, "Charisma, Migration, and Elite Coalescence," p. 428.

6. Pandolfi, "17 de octubre, trampa y salida," p. 23; T. S. Di Tella, *El sistema político argentino y la clase obrera*, pp. 10, 40; Germani, *Política y sociedad en una época de transición*, p. 324; Germani, *Estructura social de la Argentina*, pp. 76–77; Butler, "Charisma, Migration, and Elite Coalescence," p. 428; Parera Dennis, "Apuntes para una historia del peronismo," p. 13; Carri, *Sindicatos y poder en la Argentina*, p. 48; Fayt, *La naturaleza del peronismo*, pp. 70, 86; Geltman, "Mitos, símbolos, y héroes en el peronismo," p. 123; Rubinstein, "El peronismo y la vida argentina," p. 7; García Zamor, "Justicialismo en la Argentina," p. 5–6; Snow, *Political Forces in Argentina*, pp. 99–100.

7. Fayt, *La naturaleza del peronismo*, p. 86; Fillol, *Social Factors in Economic Development*, p. 83.

8. Speech by Juan Perón, 19 January 1947, quoted in Fernández, *La Unión Ferroviaria a través del tiempo*, p. 7.

9. For further discussion of this issue, see Cornelius, "The Political Sociology of Cityward Migration in Latin America."

10. Rubenstein, "El peronismo y la vida argentina," p. 7.

11. The quotation is from Whitaker, *Argentina*, p. 107. See also Fillol, *Social Factors in Economic Development*, p. 83; Parera Dennis, "Apuntes para una historia del peronismo," p. 13; Geltman, "Mitos, símbolos, y héroes en el peronismo," p. 103; Germani, *Política y sociedad en una época de transición*, p. 324.

12. POPULATION GROWTH is a composite variable, as are the other variables printed in capital letters. These variables represent the sum of the products of each component variable's standardized score and its factor score coefficient. Beginning with Table 3.1 and continuing through Table 3.5, the component variables are listed in small type directly under the composite variable. These procedures are explained in the Appendix.

13. It is important to note that this study specifically avoids any discussion of the

political influence of rural-urban migration. There are no reliable data on migrants during the early Peronist years, and, unfortunately, the more reliable data on migrants from later periods (as, for example, the individual-level sample from the 1960 census) do not provide information on political behavior or attitudes. Since the census contains only information on interprovincial migration, it is an unreliable guide to use in estimating total migration.

14. Among the many studies linking industrialization to Peronism are Fayt, *La naturaleza del peronismo*, pp. 92–93; Whitaker, *Argentina*, p. 149; Carri, *Sindicatos y poder en la Argentina*, p. 36; O'Donnell, *Modernization and Bureaucratic-Authoritarianism*, p. 56; Díaz Alejandro, *Essays on the Economic History of the Argentine Republic*, pp. 112–13.

15. It is difficult to determine the extent to which all industrial establishments are included in these data. By law all industrial firms must report their activity to the census bureau, but it is probable that many of the smaller establishments fail to do so.

16. It should be noted here and in the following discussion that Greater Buenos Aires has experienced a truly extraordinary amount of urban sprawl, and as a result an efficient urban mass-transit system—the *colectivos*—has developed to move citizens from home to work. Because there is a considerable (but unmeasured) amount of inter-*partido* commuting, the assumption in this section—that workers live and therefore vote in the same *partido* as their place of employment—is subject to error. The data presented here should therefore be considered as suggestive rather than definitive.

17. Kaplan, *Economía y política del petróleo argentino*, p. 34; G. Di Tella and Zymelman, "Etapas del desarrollo económico argentino," pp. 184–86; Fayt, *La naturaleza del peronismo*, p. 70; Carri, *Sindicatos y poder en la Argentina*, p. 26; Germani, *Política y sociedad en una época de transición*, p. 324; Geltman, "Mitos, símbolos, y héroes en el peronismo," p. 123; Scobie, *Argentina: A City and a Nation*, p. 187.

18. Guilford, *Fundamental Statistics in Psychology and Education*, pp. 400–401. See the communication from Pfotenhauer, *American Political Science Review*, pp. 205–6.

19. Pandolfi, "17 de octubre, trampa y salida," pp. 21–28; Kaplan, *Economía y política del petróleo argentino*, p. 34; Fayt, *La naturaleza del peronismo*, pp. 92–93; Whitaker, *Argentina*, p. 149.

20. A massive literature exists to confirm the *relative* satisfaction of rural-urban migrants. See Nelson's somewhat dated but excellent *Migrants, Urban Poverty, and Instability in Developing Nations*, pp. 15–20; Cornelius, "The Political Sociology of Cityward Migration in Latin America," pp. 95–147. Speaking in terms more general than those of economic satisfaction, perhaps our contemporary understanding of the political impact of cityward migration is best described in the final paragraph of Cornelius's "Urbanization and Political Demand Making," p. 1146.

21. It is probable that the decreases for the working-class districts between 1935 and 1941 stemmed more from population growth than from actual wage cuts, as migrants continued to flood into parts of Greater Buenos Aires and exert downward pressure upon wages per capita.

22. And because they have been aggregated, they tend to bias upwardly the individual-level relationship with the Peronist vote. See Gehkle and Biehel, "Certain Effects of Grouping," pp. 169–70; Yule and Kendall, *An Introduction to the Theory of Statistics*, p. 311.

23. The format for Table 3.9 is a modified copy of Table 1 in Nie, Powell, and Prewitt, "Social Structure and Political Participation," p. 812.

24. Inkeles, "Participant Citizenship in Six Developing Countries," p. 1137; Inkeles and Smith, *Becoming Modern*.

25. Turner, "The Study of Argentine Politics through Survey Research," pp. 90–100.

CHAPTER 4

1. Butler and Stokes, *Political Change in Britain*,pp. 4–5.

2. Ibid., p. 6.

3. The index of fluidity is the intellectual offspring of Professor William Ascher, an insightful young scholar who introduced me to his methodology when we were both conducting research for our dissertations in Argentina in 1971–72. For his use of the index, see Ascher and Tarrow, "The Stability of Communist Electorates," pp. 475–99. For a methodologist's explanation of the general theory underlying the index, see Tesler, "Least Squares Estimates of Transition Probabilities," pp. 270–92.

4. Kirkpatrick, *Leader and Vanguard in Mass Society*, p. 187; Catterberg, "Political Attitudes, Social Backgrounds, and Consensus among Argentine Elites."

5. Butler and Stokes, *Political Change in Britain*, p. 437.

6. Ibid., p. 291.

CONCLUSION

1. O'Donnell, *Estado y alianzas en la Argentina, 1956–1976*, p. 1.

2. Mallon and Sourrouille, *Economic Policymaking in a Conflict Society*, pp. 5–6.

3. O'Donnell, *Estado y alianzas en la Argentina, 1956–1976*, p. 2.

4. Rock, "The Survival and Restoration of Peronism," pp. 180–81.

5. Presidencia de la Nación, *Cuentas nacionales de la República Argentina*, pp. 56–57; Leiserson, *Notes on the Process of Industrialization*, p. 41; T. S. Di Tella, *El sistema político argentino y la clase obrera*, p. 104.

6. Secretaría del Estado de Hacienda, *Costo de nivel de vida en la Capital Federal*, pp. 14–16; Secretaría de Planeamiento, *Costo de vida*, p. 6.

7. Wynia, *Argentina in the Postwar Era*, p. 152.

8. Rock, "The Survival and Restoration of Peronism," p. 193.

9. Luna, *El 45: crónica de un año decisivo*, p. 44.

10. O'Donnell, *El 'juego imposible': competición y coaliciones entre partidos políticos en la Argentina*.

11. Olivieri, *Dos veces rebelde*, pp. 26–27.

12. Fodor, "Perón's Policies for Agricultural Exports," pp. 140–45.

13. O'Donnell, *Estado y alianzas en la Argentina, 1956–1976*, p. 14.

APPENDIX

1. Gehkle and Biehel, *Journal of the American Statistical Association Supplement*, pp. 169–70.

2. Yule and Kendall, *An Introduction to the Theory of Statistics*, p. 311.

3. Robinson, "Ecological Correlations and the Behavior of Individuals," p. 353.

4. Ibid., p. 354.

5. Ibid., p. 357.

6. Ranney, "The Utility and Limitations of Aggregate Data in the Study of Electoral Behavior," p. 100. See also Shively, " 'Ecological Inference,' " pp. 1183–96; Carl Lewis Taylor, *Aggregate Data Analysis*.

7. There has been substantial debate over the use of aggregate data in analyses of Argentine electoral behavior. For a sampling see Germani, "El surgimiento del peronismo," p. 435–88; Smith, "Las elecciones argentinas de 1946 y las inferencias ecológicas," p. 385–98; Kenworthy, "Interpretaciones ortodoxas y revisionistas del apoyo inicial del peronismo," pp. 749–63; Halperín Donghi, "Algunas observaciones sobre Germani, el surgimiento del peronismo y los migrantes internos," pp. 765–81.

8. Martínez Estrada, *Radiografía de la pampa*, p. 30.

9. Not everyone shares this evaluation. See Germani, "El surgimiento del peronismo," pp. 437–38.

BIBLIOGRAPHY

Albrieu, Oscar E. *Tres revoluciones: los últimos veintiocho años*. Buenos Aires: Emilio Perrot, 1959.

Alexander, Robert J. *Labor Relations in Argentina, Brazil, and Chile*. New York: McGraw-Hill, 1962.

———. *Organized Labor in Latin America*. New York: Free Press, 1965.

———. *The Perón Era*. New York: Columbia University Press, 1951.

Argentine Election Factbook, July 7, 1963. Washington, D.C.: Institute for the Comparative Study of Political Systems. 1963.

Ascher, William, and Tarrow, Sidney. "The Stability of Communist Electorates: Evidence from a Longitudinal Analysis of French and Italian Aggregate Data." *American Journal of Political Science* 19 (August 1975): 475–99.

Badanelli, Pedro. *Comunismo o justicialismo*. Santa Fe, Argentina: n.p., 1951.

Bagú, Sergio. *Evolución histórica de la estratificación social en la Argentina*. Caracas: Instituto de Investigaciones Económicas y Sociales, 1969.

Baily, Samuel L. *Labor, Nationalism, and Politics in Argentina*. New Brunswick, N.J.: Rutgers University Press, 1967.

Baldassarre, Pedro B. *El justicialismo frente al comunismo*. Buenos Aires: El Ateneo, 1951.

Ballesteros, Marta A. "Argentine Agriculture, 1908–1954: A Study in Growth and Decline." Ph.D. dissertation, University of Chicago, 1958.

Banco Central, República Argentina. *La evolución del balance de pagos de la República Argentina*. Buenos Aires: Banco Central, 1952.

Banco de la Nación, República Argentina. *Encuesta sobre inmigración*. Buenos Aires: Banco de la Nación, 1946.

Barager, Joseph R. *Why Perón Came to Power: The Background to Peronism in Argentina*. New York: Knopf, 1968.

Barrios, Américo. *Con Perón en el exilio*. Buenos Aires: Trienta Dias, 1964.

Beals, Carleton. "Argentina vs. the United States." *Current History* 50 (July 1939): 28–31.

Beveraggi Allende, Walter. *El partido laborista, el fracaso de Perón, y el problema argentino*, 2nd ed. Buenos Aires: n.p., 1956.

Blalock, Hubert M., Jr. *Causal Inferences in Non-experimental Research*. Chapel Hill: University of North Carolina Press, 1961.

———. *Causal Models in the Social Sciences*. Chicago: Aldine Atherton, 1971.

———. *Social Statistics*. New York: McGraw-Hill, 1960.

Blanksten, George I. *Perón's Argentina*. Chicago: University of Chicago Press, 1953.

Borroni, Otelo, and Vacca, Roberto. *La vida de Eva Perón. Tomo I: testimonios para su historia*. Buenos Aires: Galerna, 1970.

Braden, Spruille. "The Germans in Argentina." *Atlantic Monthly* 177 (April 1946): 37–43.

Butler, David, and Stokes, Donald. *Political Change in Britain: Forces Shaping Electoral Choice*. London: Macmillan, 1969.

Butler, David J. "Charisma, Migration, and Elite Coalescence: An Interpretation of Peronism." *Comparative Politics* 1 (April 1969): 423–39.

Cacopardo, María Cristina. *República Argentina: cambios en los límites nacionales, provinciales y departamentales, a través de los censos nacionales de población.* Documento de Trabajo no. 47. Buenos Aires: Instituto Di Tella, 1967.

Campbell, Angus; Converse, Philip E.; Miller, Warren E.; and Stokes, Donald E. *The American Voter.* New York: John Wiley, 1960.

————. *Elections and the Political Order.* New York: Wiley, 1966.

Campobassi, José S. *Los partidos políticos: estructura y vigencia en la Argentina.* Buenos Aires: Cooperadora de Derecho y Ciencias Sociales, 1963.

Canitrot, Adolfo. *La viabilidad económica de la democracia: un análisis de la experiencia peronista 1973–1976.* Buenos Aires: Estudios Sociales Cedes, 1978.

Cantón, Darío. *Materiales para el estudio de la sociología política en la Argentina.* 2 vols. Buenos Aires: Instituto Di Tella, 1968.

————. *El parlamento argentino en épocas de cambio: 1890, 1916, y 1964.* Buenos Aires: Instituto Di Tella, 1966.

————. *Party Alignments in Argentina between 1912 and 1955.* Documento de Trabajo no. 31. Buenos Aires: Instituto Di Tella, 1967.

Cárdenas, Gonzalo. *El peronismo.* Buenos Aires: Carlos Pérez, 1969.

Carri, Roberto. *Sindicatos y poder en la Argentina.* Buenos Aires: Sudestada, 1967.

Castagno, Antonio. *Tendencias y grupos políticos en la realidad argentina.* Buenos Aires: Eudeba, 1971.

Catterberg, Edgardo. "Political Attitudes, Social Backgrounds, and Consensus among Argentine Elites." Ph.D. dissertation, University of North Carolina, 1973.

Cerrutti Costa, Luis B. *El sindicalismo: las masas y el poder.* Buenos Aires: Trafac, 1957.

Chambers, E. J. "Some Factors in the Deterioration of Argentina's External Position, 1946–1951." *Inter-American Affairs* 8 (Winter 1954): 27–62.

"Church and State in Argentina: Factors in Perón's Downfall." *World Today* 12 (February 1956): 58–66.

Ciria, Alberto. "La doctrina peronista y sus fuentes." *Mundo Nuevo,* no. 47 (May 1970): 16–29.

————. *Partidos y poder en la Argentina (1930–1946).* 2nd ed. Buenos Aires: Jorge Alvarez, 1968.

————. *Perón y el justicialismo.* Buenos Aires: Siglo Veintiuno, 1971.

Comisión Coordinadora de Entidades Agropecuarias. "Salario real y política de salarios en la Argentina en 1950–65." Mimeographed. Buenos Aires: n.p., 1966.

Comisión de Prensa del Partido Socialista. "Hace un año clausuraron los tallares de *La Vanguardia,* pero el socialismo no muere." Mimeographed. Buenos Aires: Partido Socialista, 1948.

Comisión Económica para América Latina, Naciones Unidas. *Análisis y proyecciones del desarrollo económico: V, el desarrollo económico de la Argentina.* 3 vols. Mexico City: United Nations, 1959.

————. *La distribución del ingreso en América Latina.* New York: United Nations, 1970.

————. *El proceso de industrialización en América Latina.* New York: United Nations, 1965.

Comisión Nacional de Investigaciones. *Libro negro de la segunda tiranía.* Buenos Aires: Presidencia de la República, 1958.

Comisión Nacional del Censo Industrial. *Censo industrial de 1935.* Buenos Aires: Ministerio de Hacienda, 1937.

Comité Interamericano de Desarrollo Agrícola. *Tenencia de la tierra y desarrollo socioeconómico del sector agrícola: Argentina.* Washington, D.C.: Unión Panamericana, 1966.

Congress of Industrial Organizations. *The Argentine Regime: Facts and Recommendations to the United Nations Organization*. New York: Congress of Industrial Organizations, 1946.

Consejo Nacional de Desarrollo, República Argentina. *Distribución del ingreso y cuentas nacionales en la Argentina*. Buenos Aires: Conade, 1965.

Consejo Nacional de Educación, República Argentina. *IV censo escolar de la Nación*. 4 vols. Buenos Aires: Consejo Nacional de Educación, 1948.

Consejo Nacional de Postguerra. *Ordenamiento económico-social*. Buenos Aires: Consejo Nacional de Postguerra, 1945.

Constitución de la nación argentina, sancionada el 11 de marzo de 1949. Buenos Aires: n.p., 1949.

Convención Nacional Constituyente. *Diario de sesiones*. 2 vols. Buenos Aires: Convención Nacional Constituyente, 1949.

Cornelius, Wayne A., Jr. "The Political Sociology of Cityward Migration in Latin America: Toward Empirical Theory." In *Latin American Urban Research*, vol. 1, edited by Francine F. Rabinowitz and Felicity Trueblood, pp. 95–147. Beverly Hills: Sage Publications, 1971.

———. "Urbanization and Political Demand Making: Political Participation among the Migrant Poor in Latin American Cities." *American Political Science Review* 68 (September 1974): 1125–46.

———. "Urbanization as an Agent in Latin American Political Instability: The Case of Mexico." *American Political Science Review* 63 (September 1969): 833–57.

Dalto, Juan Carlos. *Crisis y auges en la economía argentina*. Buenos Aires: Macchi, 1967.

David, Pedro R. "The Social Structure of Argentina." Ph.D. dissertation, Indiana University, 1962.

de Imaz, José Luis. *La clase alta de Buenos Aires*. Buenos Aires: Instituto de Sociología, Universidad de Buenos Aires, 1965.

———. *Los que mandan (Those Who Rule)*. Translated by Carlos A. Astiz with Mary F. McCarthy. Albany: State University of New York Press, 1970.

del Mazo, Gabriel. *Breve historia del radicalismo*. Buenos Aires: Coepla, 1964.

Departamento Electoral, República Argentina. *Resultados electorales por distrito: 28-II-1965, 7-III-1965, 14-III-1965*. Buenos Aires, Ministerio del Interior, 1965.

Departamento Nacional del Trabajo, División de Estadística, República Argentina. *Organización sindical: asociaciones obreras y patronales*. Buenos Aires: Ministerio del Interior, 1941.

Department of State, United States. *Consultation among the American Republics with Respect to the Argentine Situation*. Washington, D.C.: Government Printing Office, 1946.

Deutsch, Karl W. "Social Mobilization and Political Development." *American Political Science Review* 55 (September 1961): 493–514.

Díaz Alejandro, Carlos F. *Essays on the Economic History of the Argentine Republic*. New Haven: Yale University Press, 1970.

———. *Exchange Rate Devaluation in a Semi-Industrialized Country: The Experience of Argentina, 1955–1961*. Cambridge: MIT Press, 1965.

———. "An Interpretation of Argentine Economic Growth since 1930." *Journal of Development Studies* 3 (1966–67): 14–41, 155–77.

Díaz de Vivar, Joaquín. *Orígenes de la argentinidad y nuestra revolución nacional peronista*. Madrid: Instituto de Cultura Hispánica, 1947.

Dirección de Estadística Social, República Argentina. *Evolución de los salarios, 1943–*

1945. Buenos Aires: Dirección de Estadística Social, 1946.

―――. *El índice del costo de la vida: variación de precios de artículos y servicios de primera necesidad. Tablas básicas de salarios, adaptación a la fluctuaciones del costo de la vida.* Buenos Aires: Dirección de Estadística Social, 1945.

―――. *Investigaciones sociales, 1943–1945.* Buenos Aires: Dirección de Estadística Social, 1946.

Dirección General de Estadística, República Argentina. *Anuario estadístico de la República Argentina, 1948: tomo I, compendio.* Buenos Aires: Dirección General de Estadística, 1951.

Dirección General de Estadística y Censos de la Nación, República Argentina. *Estadística industrial de 1941.* Buenos Aires: Dirección General de Estadística y Censos de la Nación, 1944.

―――. *Informe demográfico de la República Argentina, 1944–1954.* Buenos Aires: Dirección General de Estadística y Censos de la Nación, 1956.

Di Tella, Guido, and Zymelman, Manuel. "Etapas del desarrollo económico argentino." In *Argentina, sociedad de masas,* edited by Torcuato S. Di Tella, pp. 177–95. Buenos Aires: Eudeba, 1965.

Di Tella, Torcuato S., ed. *Argentina, sociedad de masas.* Buenos Aires: Eudeba, 1965.

―――. "Ideologías monolíticas en sistemas pluripartidistas: el caso latinoamericano." In *Argentina, sociedad de masas,* edited by Torcuato S. Di Tella, pp. 272–84. Buenos Aires: Eudeba, 1965.

―――. "Populism and Reform in Latin America." In *Obstacles to Change in Latin America,* edited by Claudio Véliz, pp. 47–74. London: Oxford University Press, 1965.

―――. *El sistema político argentino y la clase obrera.* Buenos Aires: Eudeba, 1964.

Diz, Adolfo C. "Money and Prices in Argentina, 1935–1962." Ph.D. dissertation, University of Chicago, 1966.

Dodson, Michael. "Priests and Peronism: Radical Clergy in Argentine Politics." *Latin American Perspectives* 1 (fall 1974): 58–72.

Dorfman, Adolfo. *Historia de la industria argentina.* Buenos Aires: Escuela de Estudios Argentinos, 1942.

Drosdoff, Daniel. *El gobierno de las vacas (1933–1956): tratado Roca-Runciman.* Buenos Aires: La Bastilla, 1972.

Dunne, Peter Masten, S. J. "Church and State in Argentina." *Review of Politics* 7 (October 1945): 395–417.

Fayt, Carlos S. *La naturaleza del peronismo.* Buenos Aires: Viracocha, 1967.

―――. *El político armado: dinámica del proceso político argentino (1960–1971).* Buenos Aires: Pannedille, 1971.

Fernández, Julio A. *The Political Elite in Argentina.* New York: New York University Press, 1970.

Fernández, Manuel F. *La Unión Ferroviaria a través del tiempo: veinticinco años al servicio de un ideal, 1922–1947.* Buenos Aires: n.p., 1947.

Ferns, H. S. *Argentina.* New York: Praeger, 1969.

Ferrer, Aldo. *The Argentine Economy.* Translated by Marjory M. Urquidi. Berkeley: University of California Press, 1967.

Figuerola, José M. F. L. *¡Preso!* Buenos Aires: n.p., 1958.

Fillol, Tomás Roberto. *Social Factors in Economic Development: The Argentine Case.* Cambridge: MIT Press, 1961.

Filosofía peronista. Buenos Aires: Mundo Peronista, 1954.

Finer, S. E. "Military and Society in Latin America." *Sociological Review Monograph* 11 (February 1967): 333–51.

Fisk, Ysabel. "Argentina: The Thirteen-Year Crisis." *Foreign Affairs* 22 (January 1942): 256–66.

Fodor, Jorge. "Perón's Policies for Agricultural Exports, 1946–1948: Dogmatism or Commonsense?" In *Argentina in the Twentieth Century*, edited by David Rock, pp. 135–61. Pittsburgh: University of Pittsburgh Press, 1975.

Forni, Floreal H., and Weinberg, Pedro D. "Reflexiones sobre la relación entre clases sociales y partidos políticos en la Argentina," *Desarrollo Económico* 12 (July–September 1972): 422–36.

Freels, John William, Jr. *El sector industrial en la política nacional.* Translated by Martha S. Gil Montero. Buenos Aires: Eudeba, 1970.

Frondizi, Arturo, *Programa de estabilización para la economía argentina: verdad, trabajo y grandeza.* Buenos Aires: Presidencia de la Nación, 1958.

Galarza, Ernesto. "Argentine Labor under Perón." *Inter-American Reports*, no. 2 (March 1948): 1–2.

Gallo, Ezequiel. *Agrarian Expansion and Industrial Development in Argentina (1880–1930).* Documento de Trabajo no. 70. Buenos Aires: Instituto Di Tella, 1970.

Gambini, Hugo, *El 17 de octubre de 1945.* Buenos Aires: Brújula, 1969.

García-Zamor, Jean-Claude. "Justicialismo en Argentina: la ideología política de Juan Domingo Perón." Mimeographed. Austin: Department of Government, University of Texas, n.d.

————. *Public Administration and Social Change in Argentina, 1943–1955.* Rio de Janeiro: Mory, 1968.

Gehkle, C. E., and Biehel, Katherine. "Certain Effects of Grouping upon the Size of the Correlation Coefficient in Census Tract Material." *Journal of the American Statistical Association*, supplement 29 (1934): 168–70.

Geltman, Pedro. "Mitos, símbolos, y héroes en el peronismo." In *El peronismo*, edited by Gonzalo Cárdenas, pp. 109–37. Buenos Aires: Carlos Pérez, 1969.

Germani, Gino. *Estructura social de la Argentina: análisis estadístico.* Buenos Aires: Raigal, 1955.

————. "Mass Immigration and Modernization in Argentina." *Studies in Comparative International Development* 2 (1966): 164–82.

————. "Mass Society, Social Class, and the Emergence of Fascism." In *Masses in Latin America*, edited by Irving L. Horowitz, pp. 577–600. New York: Oxford University Press, 1970.

————. *Política y sociedad en una época de transición: de la sociedad tradicional a la sociedad de masas.* 4th ed. Buenos Aires: Paidos, 1971.

————. "El surgimiento del peronismo: el rol de los obreros y de los migrantes internos." *Desarrollo Económico* 13 (October–December 1973): 435–88.

Goldwert, Marvin. "Dichotomies of Militarism in Argentina." *Orbis* 10 (fall 1966): 930–39.

————. "The Rise of Modern Militarism in Argentina." *Hispanic American Historical Review* 49 (May 1969): 233–53.

Green, David. *The Containment of Latin America.* Chicago: Quadrangle Books, 1971.

Greenup, Ruth, and Greenup, Leonard. *Revolution before Breakfast: Argentina, 1941–1946.* Chapel Hill: University of North Carolina Press, 1947.

Guilford, J. P. *Fundamental Statistics in Psychology and Education*, 4th ed. New York: McGraw-Hall, 1965.

Halperín Donghi, Tulio. "Algunas observaciones sobre Germani, el surgimiento del peronismo y los migrantes internos." *Desarrollo Económico* 14 (January–March 1975): 765–81.

———. "Del fascismo al peronismo," *Contorno,* no. 7–8 (July 1956): 15–21.

Hannan, Michael T. *Problems of Aggregation and Disaggregation in Sociological Research.* Working Papers in Methodology no. 4. Chapel Hill: Institute for Research in Social Science, University of North Carolina, 1970.

Hardy, Marcos Armando. *Esquema del estado justicialista: su doctrina e instituciones políticas y jurídicas.* Buenos Aires: Quetzal, 1957.

Hennessy, Alistair. "Latin America." In *Populism: Its Meaning and National Characteristics,* edited by Ghita Ionescu and Ernest Gellner, pp. 28–61. London: Weidenfeld and Nicolson, 1969.

Hodges, Donald C. *Argentina, 1943–1976: The National Revolution and Resistance.* Albuquerque: University of New Mexico Press, 1976.

Hoffmann, Fritz L. "Perón and After." *Hispanic American Historical Review* 36 (1956): 510–28.

Hoopes, Paul R. "The Problem of Cross National Comparisons: A Methodological Note on Social Research in Argentina." *Sociology and Social Research* 53 (July 1969): 475–81.

Huerta Palau, Pedro. *Análisis electoral de una ciudad en desarrollo: Córdoba, 1929–1957–1963.* Córdoba: Universidad Nacional de Córdoba, 1963.

Huntington, Samuel P. *Political Order in Changing Societies.* New Haven: Yale University Press, 1968.

Ilsley, Lucretia L. "The Argentine Constitutional Revision of 1949." *Journal of Politics* 14 (May 1952): 224–40.

Ingenieros, José. *Sociología argentina.* Buenos Aires: Losada, 1946.

Inkeles, Alex. "Participant Citizenship in Six Developing Countries." *American Political Science Review* 63 (September 1969): 1120–41.

———, and Smith, David. *Becoming Modern: Individual Change in Six Developing Countries.* Cambridge: Harvard University Press, 1974.

Instituto Nacional de Estadística y Censos, República Argentina. *Censo nacional económico 1963.* 13 vols. Buenos Aires: Instituto Nacional de Estadística y Censos, n.d.

———. *Censo nacional de población, familias, y viviendas–1970: resultados provisionales.* Buenos Aires: Instituto Nacional de Estadística y Censos, 1971.

———. *Indices del costo de nivel de vida desde febrero de 1962.* Buenos Aires: Instituto Nacional de Estadística y Censos, 1970.

Ionescu, Ghita, and Gellner, Ernest, eds. *Populism: Its Meaning and National Characteristics.* London: Weidenfeld and Nicolson, 1969.

James, Daniel. "The Peronist Left, 1955–1975." *Journal of Latin American Studies* 8 (1976): 273–96.

———. "Power and Politics in Peronist Trade Unions." *Journal of Inter-American Studies and World Affairs* 20 (February 1978): 3–36.

Jelin, Elizabeth. "Conflictos laborales en la Argentina, 1973–1976." *Revista Mexicana de Sociología* 40 (1978): 421–63.

Johnson, Dale L. "Populism, Reaction, and Revolution in Latin America." Paper presented at the 1970 annual meeting of the American Sociological Association.

Johnson, Kenneth F., in collaboration with Fuentes, María Mercedes, and Paris, Phillip L. *Argentina's Mosaic of Discord, 1966–1968.* Washington, D.C.: Institute for the Comparative Study of Political Systems, 1969.

Josephs, Ray. *Argentine Diary: The Inside Story of the Coming of Fascism*. New York: Wiley, 1944.

Junta Electoral de la Capital Federal, República Argentina. *Elecciones de convencionales constituyentes, 28 de julio de 1957*. Buenos Aires: Junta Electoral de la Capital Federal, 1957.

Junta Electoral Nacional de la Capital Federal, República Argentina. *Actas de las elecciones nacionales y municipales, 14 de marzo de 1965*. Buenos Aires: Junta Electoral Nacional de la Capital Federal, 1965.

Junta Electoral Nacional y Municipal de la Capital Federal, República Argentina. *Actas de la Junta Electoral Nacional y Municipal de la Capital Federal*. Buenos Aires: Junta Electoral Nacional y Municipal de la Capital Federal, 1960.

_____. *Actas de la Junta Electoral Nacional y Municipal de la Capital Federal*. 3 vols. Buenos Aires: Junta Electoral Nacional y Municipal de la Capital Federal, 1962.

Junta Escrutadora Nacional, República Argentina. *Actuaciones de la Junta Electoral de la Capital Federal, años 1951 a 1954*. Buenos Aires: Junta Escrutadora Nacional, 1954.

Kaplan, Marcos. *Economía y política del petróleo argentino (1939–1956)*. Buenos Aires: Praxis, 1957.

Kennedy, John J. *Catholicism, Nationalism and Democracy in Argentina*. Notre Dame: University of Notre Dame Press, 1958.

Kenworthy, Eldon. *Coalitions in the Political Development of Latin America*. Cornell University Latin American Studies Program Reprint no. 32. Ithaca: Cornell University, n.d.

_____. "Did the 'New Industrialists' Play a Significant Role in the Formation of Perón's Coalition, 1943–1946?" In *New Perspectives on Modern Argentina*, edited by Alberto Ciria, pp. 15–28. Bloomington: Indiana University Latin American Studies Program, 1972.

_____. "Interpretaciones ortodoxas y revisionistas del apoyo inicial del peronismo." *Desarrollo Económico* 14 (January–March 1975): 749–63.

Kirkpatrick, Jeane. *Leader and Vanguard in Mass Society: A Study of Peronist Argentina*. Cambridge: MIT Press, 1971.

"La era de Perón," *Panorama*, no. 27 (August 1965): 118–44.

Land, Kenneth C. "Principles of Path Analysis." In *Sociological Methodology 1969*, edited by Edgar F. Borgatta, pp. 3–37. San Francisco: Jossey-Bass, 1969.

Landenberger, Jorge W., and Conte, Francisco M. *Unión Cívica: su origin, organización y tendencias*. Buenos Aires: n.p., 1890.

Landi, Oscar. "Argentina 1973–76: la génesis de una nueva crisis política." *Revista Mexicana de Sociología* 41 (1979): 89–127.

_____. "La tercera presidencia de Perón: gobierno de emergencia y crisis política." *Revista Mexicana de Sociología* 40 (1978): 1353–1410.

Latin American Election Factsheet: Argentina. Congressional Elections, March 14, 1965. Washington, D.C.: Institute for the Comparative Study of Political Systems, 1965.

Lazarsfeld, Paul F.; Berelson, Bernard; and Gaudet, H. *The People's Choice*. New York: Columbia University Press, 1944.

Lee, Manwoo. "Argentine Political Instability: A Crisis of Simultaneous Quest for Authority and Equality." *Journal of Inter-American Studies* 11 (October 1969): 558–70.

Leiserson, Alcira. *Notes on the Process of Industrialization in Argentina, Chile, and Peru*.

Berkeley: Institute of International Studies, University of California, 1966.

Lewis, Paul H. "The Female Vote in Argentina, 1958–1965." *Comparative Political Studies* 3 (January 1971): 425–41.

Little, Walter. "The Popular Origins of Peronism." In *Argentina in the Twentieth Century*, edited by David Rock, pp. 162–78. Pittsburgh: University of Pittsburgh Press, 1975.

Llambías, Joaquín. "El salario real y la distribución del ingreso." *Panorama de la Economía* 4 (1969): 177–82.

Luna, Félix. *El 45: crónica de un año decisivo*. Buenos Aires: Sudamericana, 1971.

McGann, Thomas F. *Argentina: The Divided Land*. New York: Van Nostrand, 1966.

Mallon, Richard D., and Sourrouille, Juan V. *Economic Policymaking in a Conflict Society: The Argentine Case*. Cambridge: Harvard University Press, 1975.

Martínez Estrada, Ezequiel. *Radiografía de la pampa*. 3rd ed., 2 vols. Buenos Aires: Losada, 1946.

Martz, John D. *Acción Democrática: Evolution of a Modern Political Party in Venezuela*. Princeton: Princeton University Press, 1966.

Matthews, Herbert L. "Juan Perón's War with the Catholic Church." *Reporter* 12 (16 June 1955): 19–22.

Melo, Carlos R. *Los partidos políticos argentinos*. Córdoba: Universidad Nacional de Córdoba, 1964.

Mendé, Raúl A. *El justicialismo: doctrina y realidad peronista*. Buenos Aires: Mundo Peronista, 1950.

Merkx, Gilbert. "Sectoral Clashes and Political Change: The Argentine Experience." *Latin American Research Review* 4 (fall 1969): 89–114.

Milbrath, Lester. *Political Participation*. Chicago: Rand McNally, 1965.

Ministerio de Asuntos Económicos, República Argentina. *Régimen para las inversiones de capital extranjero*. Buenos Aires: Ministerio de Asuntos Económicos, 1953.

Ministerio de Asuntos Técnicos, República Argentina. *IV censo general de la Nación*. 3 vols. Buenos Aires: Ministerio de Asuntos Técnicos, 1952.

Ministerio de Hacienda, República Argentina, *Informe demográfico de la República Argentina*. Buenos Aires: Ministerio de Hacienda, 1956.

Ministerio de Relaciones Exteriores y Culto, República Argentina. *Junta de vigilancia y disposición final de la propiedad enemiga. Síntesis de·la labor realizada desde su creación hasta el 15 de enero de 1946*. Buenos Aires: Ministerio de Relaciones Exteriores y Culto, 1946.

Municipalidad de la Ciudad de Buenos Aires, República Argentina. *Cuarto censo general 1936: población 22-X-1936*. Buenos Aires: Municipalidad de la Ciudad de Buenos Aires, 1939.

Murkland, Harry B. "Argentine Battleground." *Current History* 9 (October 1945): 299–304.

Murmis, Miguel, and Portantiero, Juan Carlos. *Crecimiento industrial y alianza de clases en la Argentina (1930–1940)*. 2nd ed. Buenos Aires: Instituto Di Tella, 1968.

Nadra, Fernando. *Perón hoy y ayer, 1971–1943*. Buenos Aires: Polémica, 1972.

Nelson, Joan M. *Migrants, Urban Poverty, and Instability in Developing Nations*. Cambridge: Center for International Affairs, Harvard University, 1969.

Nie, Norman H.; Powell, G. Bingham, Jr.; and Prewitt, Kenneth. "Social Structure and Political Participation: Developmental Relationships." *American Political Science Review* 63 (June and September 1969): 361–78, 808–32.

O'Donnell, Guillermo. *El "juego imposible": competición y coaliciones entre partidos políticos en la Argentina, 1955–1966*. Buenos Aires: Instituto Di Tella, 1972.

———. *Estado y alianzas en la Argentina, 1956–1976*. Buenos Aires: CEDES, 1976.

———. *Modernization and Bureaucratic Authoritarianism: Studies in South American Politics*. Berkeley: Institute of International Studies, University of California, 1973.

———. "Modernization and Military Coups: Theory, Comparisons, and the Argentine Case." In *Armies and Politics in Latin America*, edited by Abraham Lowenthal, pp. 197–243. New York: Holmes and Meier, 1976.

Olarra Jiménez, Rafael. *Evolución monetaria argentina*. Buenos Aires: Eudeba, 1968.

Olivieri, Aníbal O. *Dos veces rebelde*. Buenos Aires: Ediciones Sigla, 1958.

Pandolfi, Rodolfo Mario. "17 de octubre, trampa y salida." *Contorno*, no. 7–8 (July 1956): 21–28.

Panettieri, José. *Síntesis histórica del desarrollo industrial argentina*. Buenos Aires: Macchi, 1969.

Parera Dennis, Alfredo. "Apuntes para una historia del peronismo." *Fichas* 2 (October 1965): 3–46.

Pavón Pereyra, Enrique. *Perón, preparación de una vida para el mando (1895–1942)*. 6th ed. Buenos Aires: Espino, 1952.

Pedreiro, Manuel, and Santana, Pablo. "Argentina: fracaso y empate militar." *Mundo Nuevo*, no. 53 (November 1970): 10–18.

Pendle, George. *Argentina*. London: Oxford University Press, 1963.

Perón, Eva María Duarte de. *Historia del peronismo*. Buenos Aires: Presidencia de la Nación, Subsecretaría de Informaciones, 1953.

———. *La razón de mi vida*. Buenos Aires: Peuser, 1951.

Perón, Juan Domingo. *Conducción política*. Buenos Aires: Presidencia de la Nación, Subsecretaría de Informaciones, 1954.

———. *La hora de los pueblos*. Buenos Aires: Norte, 1968.

———. *La traición de los dirigentes de la FOTIA y la FEIA a los trabajadores del azúcar*. Buenos Aires: n.p., 1949.

Peterson, Harold F. *Argentina and the United States, 1810–1960*. Albany: State University of New York Press, 1964.

Peyrou, Alejandro A., and Villanueva, Ernesto F. "Documentos para la historia del peronismo." In *El peronismo*, edited by Gonzalo Cárdenas, pp. 187–338. Buenos Aires: Carlos Pérez, 1969.

Pfotenhauer, David. "Communication." *American Political Science Review* 68 (March 1974): 205–6.

Portantiero, Juan Carlos, and Murmis, Miguel. *El movimiento obrero en los orígenes del peronismo*. Documento de Trabajo no. 57. Buenos Aires: Instituto Di Tella, 1969.

Potash, Robert A. "Argentina's Quest for Stability." *Current History* 42 (February 1962): 71–76.

———. "Argentine Political Parties." *Journal of Inter-American Studies* 1 (October 1959): 515–24.

———. "The Changing Role of the Military in Argentina." *Journal of Inter-American Studies* 3 (October 1961): 571–78.

Prebisch, Raúl. *Comentarios sobre el informe preliminar*. Buenos Aires: Secretaría de Prensa de la Presidencia de la Nación, 1955.

———. *Informe preliminar acerca de la situación económica*. Buenos Aires: Secretaría de Prensa de la Presidencia de la Nación, 1955.

———. *La situación económica del país*. Buenos Aires: Secretaría de Prensa de la Presidencia de la Nación, 1955.

Presidencia de la Nación, República Argentina. *Cuentas nacionales de la República Argentina*. Buenos Aires: Conade, 1964.

Prewitt, Kenneth. "Political Socialization and Leadership Selection." *Annals of the American Academy of Political and Social Science* 361 (September 1965): 96–111.

Puiggrós, Rodolfo. *El peronismo: sus causas*. 2nd ed. Buenos Aires: Carlos Pérez, 1971.

Rabinovitz, Bernardo. *Sucedió en la Argentina (1943–1956): lo que no se dijo*. Buenos Aires: Gure, 1956.

Ranis, Peter. "*Peronismo* without Perón: Ten Years after the Fall (1955–1965)." *Journal of Inter-American Studies* 8 (January 1966): 112–28.

Ranney, Austin. "The Utility and Limitations of Aggregate Data in the Study of Electoral Behavior." In *Essays on the Behavioral Study of Politics*, edited by Austin Ranney, pp. 91–102. Urbana: University of Illinois Press, 1962.

Reca, Lucio. "The Price and Production Duality within Argentine Agriculture, 1923–1965." Ph.D. dissertation, University of Chicago, 1967.

Recchini de Lattes, Zulma L., and Lattes, Alfredo E. *Migraciones en la Argentina: estudio de las migraciones internas e internacionales, basado en datos censales, 1869–1960*. Buenos Aires: Instituto Di Tella, 1969.

Rennie, Ysabel F. *The Argentine Republic*. New York: Macmillan, 1945.

Reportaje a la Argentina, 1943–1955. Buenos Aires: Alfredo Dupuy, 1968.

Robinson, W. S. "Ecological Correlations and the Behavior of Individuals." *American Sociological Review* 15 (June 1950): 351–57.

Rock, David. *Politics in Argentina, 1890–1930: The Rise and Fall of Radicalism*. London: Cambridge University Press, 1975.

———. "The Survival and Restoration of Peronism." In *Argentina in the Twentieth Century*, edited by David Rock, pp. 179–221. Pittsburgh: University of Pittsburgh Press, 1975.

Rodríguez, Carlos J. *Irigoyen: su revolución política y social*. Buenos Aires: La Facultad, 1943.

Romero, José Luis. *Breve historia de la Argentina*. Buenos Aires: Eudeba, 1965.

———. *A History of Argentine Political Thought*. Translated by Thomas F. McGann. Stanford: Stanford University Press, 1963.

———. *Las ideas políticas en la Argentina*. Mexico: Fondo de Cultura Económica, 1946.

Rowe, James W. *The Argentine Elections of 1963*. Washington, D.C.: Institute for the Comparative Study of Political Systems, 1963.

Rozitchner, León. "Experiencia proletaria y experiencia burguesa." *Contorno*, no. 7–8 (July 1956): 2–8.

Rubinstein, Juan Carlos. "El peronismo y la vida argentina." *Fichas* 2 (December 1965): 3–13.

Sábato, Ernesto. *El otro rostro del peronismo: carta abierta a Mario Amadeo*. Buenos Aires: López, 1956.

Sábato, Jorge A. *SEGBA, congestión y banco mundial*. Buenos Aires: Juárez, 1971.

Sagastume, Jorge. "Nasserismo y peronismo." *Fichas* 2 (May 1966): 14–18.

Santos Gollán, José. "Argentine Interregnum." *Foreign Affairs* 35 (October 1956): 84–94.

Schoultz, Lars. *Human Rights and United States Policy toward Latin America*. Princeton: Princeton University Press, 1981.

———. "The Nature of Anti–United States Sentiment in Latin America: A Preliminary Analysis with Argentine Data." *Comparative Politics* 11 (July 1979): 467–81.

———. "Political Normlessness in Comparative Perspective." *Journal of Politics* 40 (February 1978): 82–111.

———. "The Socioeconomic Determinants of Popular-Authoritarian Electoral Behavior: The Case of Peronism." *American Political Science Review* 71 (December 1977): 1423–46.

————. "Urbanization and Political Change in Latin America." *Midwest Journal of Political Science* 16 (August 1972): 367–87.

Schwartz, Hugh H. "The Argentine Experience with Industrial Credit and Protection Incentives, 1943–1958." Ph.D. dissertation, Yale University, 1967.

Scobie, James R. *Argentina: A City and a Nation*. New York: Oxford University Press, 1964.

Sebreli, Juan José. *Buenos Aires, vida cotidiana y alienación*. 3rd ed. Buenos Aires: Siglo Veinte, 1965.

Secretaría del Estado de Hacienda, Dirección Nacional de Estadística y Censos, República Argentina. *Censo de comercio 1954*. 2 vols. Buenos Aires: Secretaría del Estado de Hacienda, 1959.

————. *Costo de nivel de vida en la Capital Federal*. 3rd ed. Buenos Aires: Secretaría del Estado de Hacienda, 1968.

Secretaría de Planeamiento y Acción de Gobierno, Instituto Nacional de Estadística y Censos. *Costo de vida*. Buenos Aires: Secretaría de Planeamiento y Acción de Gobierno, 1971.

Seligman, Lester G. "Elite Recruitment and Political Development." *Journal of Politics* 26 (August 1964): 612–26.

Senado de la Nación, República Argentina. *Extirpación del latifundio en el norte argentino*. Buenos Aires: Senado de la Nación, 1949.

Senén Gonzáles, Santiago. *El sindicalismo despues de Perón*. Buenos Aires: Balerna, 1971.

Setaro, Ricardo. "The Argentine Fly in the International Ointment." *Harper's Magazine* 189 (August 1944): 204–9.

Shils, Edward. *The Torment of Secrecy*. London: Heinemann, 1956.

Shively, W. Phillips. "'Ecological' Inference: The Use of Aggregate Data to Study Individuals." *American Political Science Review* 63 (December 1969): 1183–96.

Shklar, Judith N. *Men and Citizens: A Study of Rousseau's Social Theory*. Cambridge, Mass.: University Press, 1969.

Silenzi de Stagni, Adolfo. *El petróleo argentino*. Buenos Aires: Problemas Nacionales, 1955.

Simon, Herbert A. *Models of Man*. New York: Wiley, 1957.

Smith, Peter H. "Las elecciones argentinas de 1946 y las inferencias ecológicas." *Desarrollo Económico* 14 (July–September 1974): 385–98.

————. *Politics and Beef in Argentina: Patterns of Conflict and Change*. New York: Columbia University Press, 1969.

————. "Los radicales argentinos y la defensa de los intereses ganaderos, 1916–1930." *Desarrollo Económico* 7 (April–June 1967): 795–829.

————. "Social Mobilization, Political Participation, and the Rise of Juan Perón." *Political Science Quarterly* 84 (March 1969): 30–49.

Snow, Peter G. *Argentine Political Parties and the 1966 Revolution*. Iowa City: Laboratory for Political Research, University of Iowa, 1968.

————. *Argentine Radicalism: The History and Doctrine of the Radical Civic Union*. Iowa City: University of Iowa Press, 1965.

————. "Argentine Radicalism: 1957–1963." *Journal of Inter-American Studies* 5 (October 1963): 507–31.

————. "The Class Basis of Argentine Political Parties." *American Political Science Review* 63 (March 1969): 163–67.

————. "The Evolution of the Argentine Electoral System." *Parliamentary Affairs* 18 (summer 1965): 330–36.

————. "Parties and Politics in Argentina: The Elections of 1962 and 1963." *Midwest Journal of Political Science* 9 (February 1965): 1–36.

————. *Political Forces in Argentina*. Boston: Allyn and Bacon, 1971.

————. *Political Forces in Argentina*. Rev. ed. New York: Praeger, 1979.

————. "El político argentino." *Revista Española de la Opinión Pública* 6 (December 1966): 135–49.

Solberg, Carl. "Immigration and Urban Social Problems in Argentina and Chile, 1890–1914." *Hispanic American Historical Review* 49 (May 1969): 215–32.

Springer, Philip B. "Disunity and Disorder: Factional Politics in the Argentine Military." In *The Military Intervenes: Case Studies in Political Development*, edited by Henry Bienen, pp. 145–68. New York: Russell Sage Foundation, 1968.

Stein, Steve. *Populism in Peru: The Emergence of the Masses and the Politics of Social Control*. Madison: University of Wisconsin Press, 1980.

Stewart, Angus. "The Social Roots." In *Populism: Its Meaning and National Characteristics*, edited by Ghita Ionescu and Ernest Gellner, pp. 180–96. London: Weidenfeld and Nicolson, 1969.

Stokes, Donald E. "Compound Paths in Political Analysis." Mimeographed. Ann Arbor: Department of Political Science, University of Michigan, 1972.

Strout, Richard Robert. *The Recruitment of Candidates in Mendoza Province, Argentina*. Chapel Hill: University of North Carolina Press, 1968.

Subsecretaría de Informaciones, Dirección General del Registro Nacional, República Argentina. *Estatuto del peón*. Buenos Aires: Subsecretaría de Informaciones, 1950.

Subsecretaría de Informaciones, Ministerio del Interior, República Argentina. *Las fuerzas armadas restituyen el imperio de la soberanía popular: las elecciones generales de 1946*. 2 vols. Buenos Aires: Subsecretaría de Informaciones, 1946.

Tandy, A. H. *Argentina: Economic and Social Conditions in the Argentine Republic*. London: Her Majesty's Stationery Office, 1956.

Taylor, Carl Lewis, ed. *Aggregate Data Analysis: Political and Social Indicators in Cross National Research*. Paris: Mouton, 1968.

Tesler, Lester G. "Least Squares Estimates of Transition Probabilities." In *Measurement in Economics*, edited by Carl F. Christ, pp. 270–92. Stanford: Stanford University Press, 1963.

Tindall, George. "Populism: A Semantic Identity Crisis." *Virginia Quarterly Review* 48 (autumn 1972): 501–18.

Torres, José Luis. *La década infame*. Buenos Aires: Formación Patria, 1945.

Treber, Salvador. *La empresa estatal argentina: su gestión económico-financiera*. Buenos Aires: Macchi, 1969.

Turner, Frederick C. "The Study of Argentine Politics through Survey Research." *Latin American Research Review* 10 (summer 1975): 90–100.

Vaky, Viron P. "Hemispheric Relations: 'Everything Is Part of Everything Else.'" *Foreign Affairs* 59 (1981): 617–47.

Vapñarsky, César A. *La población urbana argentina: revisión crítica del método y los resultados censales de 1960*. Buenos Aires: Instituto Di Tella, 1968.

Véliz, Claudio. *The Centralist Tradition of Latin America*. Princeton: Princeton University Press, 1980.

Villanueva, Javier. *The Inflationary Process in Argentina, 1943–1960*. Buenos Aires: Instituto Di Tella, 1964.

Wellhofer, E. Spencer. "The Mobilization of the Periphery: Perón's 1946 Triumph." *Comparative Political Studies* 7 (July 1974): 239–51.

Whitaker, Arthur P. *Argentina*. Englewood Cliffs, N.J.: Prentice-Hall, 1964.

_____. *Argentine Upheaval: Perón's Fall and the New Regime*. New York: Praeger, 1956.

_____. "Blue Book Blues." *Current History* 10 (April 1946): 289–97.

_____. *The United States and Argentina*. Cambridge: Harvard University Press, 1954.

_____, and Jordan, David C. *Nationalism in Contemporary Latin America*. New York: Free Press, 1966.

Wiles, Peter. "A Syndrome, Not a Doctrine." In *Populism: Its Meaning and National Characteristics*, edited by Ghita Ionescu and Ernest Gellner, pp. 166–79. London: Weidenfeld and Nicolson, 1969.

World Bank. *World Development Report, 1980*. New York: Oxford University Press 1980.

Worsley, Peter. "The Concept of Populism." In *Populism: Its Meaning and National Characteristics*, edited by Ghita Ionescu and Ernest Gellner, pp. 212–50. London: Weidenfeld and Nicolson, 1969.

Wynia, Gary W. *Argentina in the Postwar Era: Politics and Economic Policy Making in a Divided Society*. Albuquerque: University of New Mexico Press, 1978.

Yule, G. Udny, and Kendall, Maurice G. *An Introduction to the Theory of Statistics*. London: Charles Griffin, 1950.

Zalduendo, Eduardo. *Geografía electoral de la Argentina*. Buenos Aires: Ancora, 1958.

Zymelman, Manuel. "The Economic History of Argentina, 1933–1952." Ph.D. dissertation, Massachusetts Institute of Technology, 1958.

INDEX

Aggregate data, 58, 67, 97–99; and ecological fallacy, 97–98
Alem, Leandro, 19
Almond, Gabriel, 44
Aprismo, 7
Aramburu, Pedro, 12, 88
Argentina: and political instability, 11; social statistics, 11; human rights violations, 12, 13; lack of democracy, 12; foreign investment, 14; immigration, 14; labor force 15; foreign trade, 15
Asociación Obrera Textil, 38

Biehel, Katherine, 97
Bignone, Reynaldo, 12
Borlenghi, Angel, 35, 37
Braden, Spruille, 92
Bramuglia, Juan Atilio, 36
Bureaucratic authoritarianism, 8
Butler, David, 67, 75

Cámpora, Héctor, 91
Carri, Roberto, 33
Castillo, Ramón, 21
Castroism, 7
Catholic church, 86–87
Composite variables, 101–2
Concentración Obrera, 22
Concordancia, 21, 22
Confederación de Trabajadores de la América Latina (CTAL), 35
Confederación Obrera Argentina, 34
Conservative party, 22
Cornelius, Wayne, 44
Council of the Americas, 86

De Imaz, José Luis, 39
Dellepiane, Luis, 92
Del Mazo, Gabriel, 92
Del Valle, Aristóbulo, 19
Depression of 1930s, 14, 91
Deutsch, Karl, 9
Dirección Nacional Electoral, 99

Diskin, David, 37
Di Tella, Torcuato S., 4–8
Domenech, José, 35, 37

Economic satisfaction: and vote for Peronism, 53–57; and electoral fluidity, 75–78
Ezeiza Airport massacre, 41

Fayt, Carlos, 36, 45
Federación de Asociaciones Católicas de Empleadas, 35
Federación Obrera Local Bonaerense, 34
Federación Obrera Regional Argentina (FORA), 34
Federación Sindical Internacional, 35
Federation of Labor Unions of the Meat Industry, 38
Federation of Sugar Industry Workers, 38
Federation of Workers of the Meat Industry, 37
Figuerola, José, 32, 89
Fillol, Tomás Roberto, 45
Fluidity: index, 68–71; and social class, 71–73; and industrialization, 73, 78–79; and urbanization, 75; and demographic instability, 75; and economic satisfaction, 75–78
Frondizi, Arturo, 90, 100
Fuerza Orientadora Radical de la Joven Argentina (FORJA), 92
Fuerzas Armadas Peronistas, 41
Fuerzas Armadas Revolucionarias, 41

Galimberti, Rodolfo, 41
Galtieri, Leopoldo, 12
Gay, Luis, 34, 37
Gehkle, Charles Elmer, 97
General Confederation of Commercial Employees, 38
General Confederation of Labor (CGT), 33, 88

General Economic Confederation, 88
Germani, Gino, 9, 17, 66
Guerrillas, 41
Guido, José María, 12
Guilford, J. P., 53

Hagen, E. E., 6, 8
Hennessy, Alistair, 5

Immigration, 14, 15; and political
   efficacy, 15; and naturalization laws,
   16; and residence in Argentina, 16;
   from neighboring countries, 16
Industrial growth, 14, 48–53, 59–65;
   and electoral fluidity, 73, 78–79
Ingenieros, José, 18
Inkeles, Alex, 44, 65

Jauretche, Arturo, 92
Johnson, Dale, 4
Juárez Celman, Miguel, 18, 94
Juventud Argentina por la Emancipa-
   ción Nacional (JAEN), 41
Juventud Peronista (JP), 41–42

Kendall, Maurice G., 97
Kirkpatrick, Jeane, 28–29

Labor movement: and Peronism,
   32–40, 89–90; historical develop-
   ment in Argentina, 34–40; strikes,
   34; ideology, 35
Labor party, 37
La Fraternidad, 35–36, 38
Lanusse, Alejandro, 12, 20
Law of Professional Associations, 39,
   88
Levingston, Roberto, 12
Liberalism: in Argentina, 13, 85–94;
   conflict with national populism, 13;
   and middle class, 86; and Catholic
   church, 86; and armed forces, 86
Lonardi, Eduardo, 12, 87–88
Lucero, Franklin, 89
Luna, Félix, 89

McGann, Thomas, 11
Mallon, Richard D., 86
Malvinas (Falkland) Islands, 13, 85

Manzi, Homero, 92
Martínez de Hoz, José, 93, 94
Martz, John, 7
Mercante, Domingo, 36, 37
Migration (internal), 14, 16, 44–45;
   reasons for, 17. *See also* Immigration
Military, 86
Mitre, Bartolomé, 18
Montoneros, 41–42
Monzalvo, Luis, 37
Movement of Third World Priests, 87

National Postwar Council, 39
Nationalism, 91–93
Nie, Norman H., 44
Nobel peace prize, 12

O'Donnell, Guillermo, 86–87, 90, 94
Olivieri, Aníbal, 92
Onganía, Juan Carlos, 12
Ongaro, Raimundo, 41

Partido Autonomista Nacional, 18
Pavón, Battle of (1861), 18
Pérez Esquivel, Adolfo, 12
Pérez Leiros, Francisco, 35
Perón, Eva María Duarte de, 3, 27
Perón, Juan, 3, 14; leadership, 3; and
   Socialist party, 24–25; and class
   struggle, 27, 35; and organized
   labor, 32–40
Perón, María Estela ("Isabel") Martínez de, 42
Peronism: and class consciousness,
   21–25, 27; components of coalition,
   25, 28–29, 40, 85; and Marxism, 27;
   and working class, 29–40, 85; and
   organized labor, 32–40; and middle
   class, 40, 85; and guerrillas, 41; and
   demographic change, 43–47, 85;
   and industrial growth, 48–53,
   59–65, 85; and economic satisfaction, 53–57; and electoral fluidity,
   79–84; and rural labor, 89–90; and
   justicialism, 93; parties comprising
   coalition, 100–101
Peter, José, 37–38
Population growth, 45–47, 65; and
   electoral fluidity, 75

Populism: in Latin America, 3–4; definition, 4; and social classes, 5; and elite recruitment, 5–6; and status incongruence, 6, 8; and radical change, 6, 8; sub-populisms, 7; structural deterrents to development, 7; as a residual category, 7; alternatives to, 8; and social mobilization, 8; in Argentina, 13, 14–18; conflict with liberalism, 13; postwar coalition in Argentina, 25

Powell, G. Bingham, Jr., 44
Prewitt, Kenneth, 8, 44
Puigbó, Raúl, 89

Radical Youth Orienting Force. *See* Fuerza Orientadora Radical de la Joven Argentina
Ranney, Austin, 98
Revolución Libertadora, 90, 100
Revolution of 1943, 34, 36
Reyes, Cipriano, 37–38, 39
Robinson, William, 97
Roca, Julio A., 18
Roca-Runciman treaty, 87
Rock, David, 87
Rockefeller, David, 86
Rojas, Ricardo, 91
Rojas Pinilla, Gustavo, 7
Rosas, Juan Manuel de, 14, 18, 88

Sábato, Ernesto, 34
Sáenz Peña, Roque, 19
Sáenz Peña law, 19, 85
Scalabrini Ortiz, Raúl, 92
Sebreli, Juan José, 28, 29
Secretaría Electoral de la Capital Federal, 99, 103
Secretariat of Labor and Welfare, 27, 32, 36
Service for Justice and Peace, 12
Shils, Edward, 4
Shively, W. Phillips, 98
Shklar, Judith, 4
Sindicato de la Industria del Calzado, 38
Smith, Peter, 21
Snow, Peter, 33

Social class: and class consciousness in Argentina, 18, 21–25; and support for Peronism, 29–42; and electoral fluidity, 71–73; defined, 102
Social Contract, 42
Socialist party, 21–25; approach to reform, 24–25
Social mobilization, 8–10, 44; defined, 9
Sourrouille, Juan V., 86
Stokes, Donald, 67, 75

Tosco, Augustín, 41

Unicato, 18, 19
Unión Cívica, 18
Unión Cívica Principista, 19
Unión Cívica Radical, 19, 85, 89, 94, 100; and reforms, 20
Unión Cívica Radical Intransigente, 100
Unión de Contribuyentes, 22
Unión Ferroviaria, 35–37, 45
Unión Obrera de la Industria del Calzado, 38
Unión Obrera Textil, 38
Union of Bakery Personnel, 38
Union of Construction Workers, 38
Union of Wood Industry Workers, 38
Unión Popular, 100
Unión Sindical Argentina (USA), 34
Urbanization, 44–46; and electoral fluidity, 75
Urquiza, Justo José de, 18, 88

Valle, Juan José, 89
Verba, Sidney, 44
Videla, Jorge Rafael, 12, 94

Wiles, Peter, 4
Worsley, Peter, 4, 40
Wynia, Gary, 42

Yacimientos Petrolíferos Fiscales (YPF), 20
Yrigoyen, Hipólito, 19, 85, 94
Yule, G. Udny, 97